Mangos, Chiles, and Truckers

CRITICAL AMERICAN STUDIES SERIES

GEORGE LIPSITZ
UNIVERSITY OF CALIFORNIA–SAN DIEGO
SERIES EDITOR

Mangos, Chiles, and Truckers

The Business of Transnationalism

Robert R. Alvarez Jr.

Critical American Studies

University of Minnesota Press
Minneapolis • London

Lines from "La Línea," by Adrian Arancibia, reprinted at the end of the Foreword with the permission of the poet.

Chapter 1 originally appeared as "Beyond the Border: Nation-State Encroachment, NAFTA, and Offshore Control in the U.S.–Mexican Mango Industry," *Human Organizations* 60, no. 2 (summer 2001): 121–27; reprinted with permission from the Society for Applied Anthropology. Chapter 2 originally appeared as "*La Maroma:* Chiles, Credit, and Chance: An Ethnographic Case of Global Finance and Middlemen Entrepreneurs," *Human Organizations* 57, no. 1 (spring 1998): 63–73; reprinted with permission from the Society for Applied Anthropology. Chapter 3 was originally published as an article coauthored with George A. Collier in *American Ethnologist* 21, no. 3 (1994): 606–27; copyright 1994 by the American Anthropological Association; reprinted with permission from the University of California Press. Chapter 5 originally appeared in *Journal of the West* 40, no. 2 (spring 2001); copyright 2001 by Journal of the West, Inc.; reprinted with permission from Journal of the West, 1531 Yuma, Manhattan, KS 66502 USA.

Copyright 2005 by the Regents of the University of Minnesota

All rights reserved. No part of this publication may be reproduced, stored in a retrieval system, or transmitted, in any form or by any means, electronic, mechanical, photocopying, recording, or otherwise, without the prior written permission of the publisher.

Published by the University of Minnesota Press
111 Third Avenue South, Suite 290
Minneapolis, MN 55401-2520
http://www.upress.umn.edu

Library of Congress Cataloging-in-Publication Data

Alvarez, Robert R.
Mangos, chiles, and truckers : the business of transnationalism / Robert R. Alvarez Jr.
p. cm. — (Critical American Studies series)
Includes bibliographical references and index.
ISBN 0-8166-4507-8 (hc : alk. paper) — ISBN 0-8166-4508-6 (pb : alk. paper)
1. United States—Commerce—Mexico. 2. Mexico—Commerce—United States.
3. Transnationalism. 4. Produce trade—Mexico. 5. Truck drivers—Mexico. I. Title. II. Series.
HF3066.A68 2005
382'.0972'073—dc22

2005004883

Printed in the United States of America on acid-free paper

The University of Minnesota is an equal-opportunity educator and employer.

12 11 10 09 08 07 06 05   10 9 8 7 6 5 4 3 2 1

In memory of Robert R. Alvarez Sr.

Contents

Foreword
The Grounded Transnationalism
of Robert Alvarez

George Lipsitz

I am new. History made me.
My first language was spanglish.
I was born at the crossroads
and I am whole.

—Aurora Levins Morales

We live in a time of rapid change and radical transformation. Traditional understandings of place, culture, work, and citizenship seem to be eroding before our eyes. The rapid movement across borders of products, people, images, and ideas alters our understanding of the nation-state and its role in our lives. New technologies enable manufacturers to spread production all over the world, while providing communications conglomerates with access to global markets. The centralized power of transnational corporations and transnational institutions like the World Bank and the International Monetary Fund overwhelms local forms of regulation and imposes uniform economic and social policies on what had previously been sovereign nations.

Yet the nation-state does not disappear under these circumstances. In fact, it becomes even more important, because, as Robert Alvarez explains in a compact phrase, "the nation-state manages transnationalism." The state channels capital to private interests. It bails out the bad loans and unwise investments of national capitalists. The nation-state underwrites the development of new technologies for transnationalism, like the Internet and computer-automated container shipping. It jails dissidents, and it maintains the unequal social conditions that force large numbers of people to migrate across borders to higher-wage countries.

In this book, Robert Alvarez provokes us to think about these processes in a new way. He asks us to view transnationalism from below, on the ground, in the ways it makes itself felt in the ordinary everyday lives of people on both sides of the U.S.–Mexico border. He demonstrates that even the most well coordinated and carefully orchestrated global policies can have surprising and unanticipated local effects. He shows us how people make meaning for themselves under circumstances they do not control, how the emergence of new forms of commerce, new patterns of migration, and new systems of social control lead people to fashion new survival strategies and create their own new forms of social identity, social alliance, and social affiliation.

Of course, transnational trade and global commerce are not new. They have been on the ascendancy since the fifteenth century. Centuries of brutal conquest, systematic exploitation, and imperial domination continue to structure relations between countries and continents. Yet, although transnationalism is not new, its present incarnation poses particularly vexing problems. The implementation of treaties like the North American Free Trade Agreement (NAFTA), the extraordinary power of transnational financial institutions, and the development of new methods of production and distribution have undermined older understandings of place, power, culture, and community. As Immanuel Wallerstein et al. argue in *Open the Social Sciences*, developments in the world since 1945 raise serious questions about the continuing utility of social-science categories that originated in the eighteenth century.[1] New social relations are creating new social subjects whose actions give rise to new archives, epistemologies, and imaginings. We need to develop new ways of knowing, new theories, and new methodologies to understand transnationalism in its present form.

Scholars thus far have tended to study transnationalism from the top down. Their work helps us see how transnationalism appears from the vantage point of corporate boardrooms, first-class cabins on jumbo jets, and the offices of national security agencies. Robert Alvarez gives us another view. He follows the mango and the chile pepper from the fields of rural Mexico to the supermarkets and dinner tables of Southern California. He studies the Mexican trucking industry in Baja California, Sonora, and Chiapas and the fruit and vegetable business in the markets of downtown Los Angeles to show how the existence and meaning of the international border orders the organization of work, community, and social space hundreds of miles away from the actual geophysical line between nations.

Perhaps most important, Alvarez shows that the transnational system does not create an undifferentiated cultural uniformity across national boundaries, but rather gives new meaning to entrenched cultural traditions, while at the same time provoking the emergence of new ones. Alvarez's investigations of the entrepreneurial logic of *la maroma* among Mexican *fruteros*, of kin and community relationships in the Mexican trucking industry, of the ethnic hierarchies in Los Angeles markets, and of "re-*mexicanidad*" in the later lives of longtime resident *mexicanos* in Lemon Grove, California, all testify to the enduring importance of cultural difference. For all the cruelty, brutality, and exploitation embedded in new transnational relations, the people Alvarez describes are not helpless. They draw on a rich array of cultural resources to make up for what they lack in wealth and political power. Yet these cultural resources are not simply there for the taking, they have to be conjured up through the active work of preservation, renewal, and, in some cases, even invention.

One of the great virtues of Alvarez's methods is the way they enable us to understand the microsocial and experiential dimensions of macrosocial systemic change. It is one thing to recognize that the United States now houses the fifth-largest population of Spanish speakers in the world, but quite another to realize that U.S. consumers now purchase more chile salsa than catsup. It is one thing to note that more than 3.7 million people of Mexican ancestry and more than 1.3 million of Asian ancestry reside in Los Angeles, but quite another to understand that half of U.S. mango sales take place in Los Angeles, and that these purchases, largely by immigrant and ethnic households, now position the

United States as the world's leading importer of mangos. Two decades ago, almost no mangos were imported into the United States. Migration-based demographic change is a cultural as well as an economic process: it transforms the supermarket as well as the labor market.

Yet there is an uneven quality to the cultural mixing engendered by transnationalism. Old and new inequalities leave diverse communities juxtaposed against one another rather than blended together smoothly into an interactive totality. Cultures clash, but they do not always coalesce. As Alvarez explains, the aggregate high volume of U.S. mango imports hides the fact that only one-third of U.S. households have ever purchased a mango, that the demand remains concentrated in immigrant and ethnic communities. Similarly, when Mexican fruit and vegetable sellers conduct business in the markets of downtown Los Angeles, they do not become undifferentiated "Americans," but rather must remain strongly invested in a Mexican identity as national subjects working in a historically and socially specific transnational space. Anti-Mexican discrimination and their low capitalization compel Mexican *fruteros* in Los Angeles to cultivate their binational identity as a business resource. They use their local and regional knowledge about both countries to secure access to the Mexican products capable of bringing the highest prices in the U.S. market. They rely on reciprocal notions of kinship obligations and extended community ties in order to gain privileged access to reliable low-wage labor. Continuing waves of immigration from Mexico supply these entrepreneurs with predictable consumer demand and new business opportunities. Consequently, although the United States imports more mangos than any country in the world, inside the United States the acquisition, distribution, and consumption of mangos takes place inside geographically limited and socially specific ethnic niche markets.

Yet this does not mean that most U.S. citizens are uninvolved in the mango trade. Alvarez shows that the U.S. nation-state and its policies shape the movement of the mango in every detail. In keeping with his argument that an important new role for the nation-state is managing transnationalism, Alvarez explains how the U.S. Department of Agriculture

(USDA) serves the interests of U.S. agribusiness by setting standards for imported mangos in such a way as to give highly capitalized U.S. firms hierarchical control over the industry. The USDA responded to a legitimate fear of fruit-fly infestation of mangos in 1987 by mandating the use of expensive hot water systems that raised capital costs for mango exporters and made them more dependent on U.S. business and capital. Deputized inspectors from the United States now serve as the "mango police" in Peru, Ecuador, Nicaragua, Guatemala, Haiti, and the Dominican Republic, and in Mexico a private company conducts inspections using standards devised by the USDA—which retains final control of certification. Consumers who have not yet purchased mangos nonetheless participate in the mango trade because their tax dollars support a hemispheric political and economic system encompassing institutions, people, and products thousands of miles from the nation's borders. These practices augment the competitive power of U.S. corporations, but in the process they also contribute to the economic inequalities that make Central American and South American mango consumers migrate to the United States in the first place. Like raids by the Border Patrol in Midwest high schools and communities far from the actual border, the activities of the USDA reveal the ways in which the U.S. nation-state's control of "the border" masks what Alvarez describes as a larger penetration into Mexico and the rest of Latin America.

The expanded reach and scope of the U.S. nation-state and the seemingly unlimited power of U.S. capital structure the contours of transnational trade. For more than two decades, structural adjustment policies favored by the United States and implemented by the World Bank and the International Monetary Fund have brought increasing inequality and austerity to people in Latin America, Africa, and Asia. These policies require countries to slash their expenditures on health, housing, education, and transportation in order to create new opportunities for investors. While corporate profits and stock values soar to unprecedented heights, more than a billion people around the globe subsist on incomes less than one dollar per day. Every day, more than thirty thousand children under the age of five die from malnutrition or

completely curable diseases. In Mexico, the twenty-four wealthiest families now have more money than the 24 million poorest Mexicans.[2] Transnational capitalism as austerity and inequality reaches every corner of
the globe.

Actual economic actors, however, never encounter transnationalism in the abstract, but rather confront *specific* transnational situations,
relations, and negotiations. Each locality inflects transnationalism with
its particularities—its history, its culture, its contradictions. These particularities can provide aggrieved communities with resources for fight-
ing back, with weapons they can use in their own defense in the arenas
that are open to them. Alvarez offers us an illustrative example of this
kind of resistance: *la maroma* as practiced by Mexican "middlemen" exporters in the chile pepper trade.

La maroma is a culturally based entrepreneurial logic based on
"floating" payments to creditors in order to gain the maximum use from
scarce capital. Alvarez explains that would-be exporters in Mexico generally lack collateral, and consequently find themselves saddled with
high-interest payments on large loans. In order to stay in business, they
must draw on their kinship and friendship networks for specific knowledge about chile harvests and local banking practices. They incur obligations by borrowing money from loan sharks, friends who work at
money-exchange houses, relatives, and other entrepreneurs. Paying back
these loans requires high-volume sales, so they need to purchase the best
chile peppers at the best prices. They rely on cell phones and extended
social networks to make purchases, even though they do not actually
have the money they are spending. They write checks that are not good
when they are written, but can become good by the time they are cashed
if the account is replenished from other sources. They buy two loads of
peppers when they only have enough money to purchase one, in the
hope that they will have sold the second load by the time payment for it
comes due. These practices entail great risks, but social networks, high-
volume sales, and knowledge of the exact amount of time each local bank
needs to clear a check enable the *chileros* to compete successfully in the
export market.

Mexican-American entrepreneurs use local knowledge about both sides of the border to their advantage. The very "free-trade" policies that create austerity in Mexico also promote the mass migration of Mexicans to the United States, where they become a lucrative market for the sale of chile peppers. Migration from Mexico also extends social and kinship networks into the United States, creating business opportunities for culturally knowledgeable Spanish speakers and producing business contacts for Mexican exporters. Although generally in an unfavorable competitive position vis-à-vis U.S. firms, there are times when Mexican exporters use their knowledge, contacts, and prowess at *la maroma* to dominate the most lucrative parts of the chile market.

Demand in the United States for chile and other Mexican vegetables and fruits shapes the contours of business and social relations across borders, but it also reconfigures local, regional, and national affiliations in Mexico itself. The chile pepper was once a local product, but high-volume demand from the United States has led to coordinated production throughout Mexico. This requires exporters to make contacts all over the republic, to use cell phones, fax machines, and other technologies to remain in constant contact with their suppliers. Regional rivalries and differences do not disappear under these circumstances, but citizenship and social membership in Mexico take on new meanings because of the new networks, circuits, and affiliations created inside the nation in response to the demands of transnational commerce.

Alvarez explores the impact of transnational trade on Mexican regional identities in his discussion of the Mexican trucking industry (coauthored with George Collier). As truckers in the north of Mexico increasingly become involved in trade with the United States, new firms have emerged in southern Mexico to ship products to and from Mexico City. *Norteño* truckers have developed new forms of patronage and personal ties to help them maximize resources and manage risk. National pride as Mexicans (and international solidarity with Mexican-Americans) provide *norteño* truckers with cultural resources that can be deployed as valuable business assets. They can use the presumption of linked fate and common destiny to establish reciprocal responsibilities and obligations.

Family ties, patronage, and trust create networks of mutual support that make Mexican trucking more profitable. Their success, in turn, creates employment and other business opportunities in the United States for Mexican-Americans capable of tapping into their networks. *Norteño* truckers thus develop a transnational understanding of Mexican identity.

Sudeño truckers, on the other hand, remain within the juridical and geographic boundaries of Mexico. They open up new interregional relations and networks, but ultimately participation in the trucking industry reinforces for them their identification as highland Mayas, more than it gives a new meaning to being Mexican. Whereas the truckers in the north are independent entrepreneurs, the southern truckers are part of organized trade unions closely connected to the Partido Revolucionario Institucional (PRI), until recently the nation's dominant political party. Most of the people involved in the trucking industry in southern Mexico are full-time farmers and only part-time truckers. They seek supplementary incomes from trucking, but remain reliant on community and ethnic contacts in the other aspects of their lives. As a result, they do not always follow the dominant market logic of transnational capital. Instead of seeking maximum rewards for themselves, they rotate opportunities among members of the group, engage in cooperative buying, and serve as a surrogate public bus system by transporting people as well as products. They enter a wider world through trucking enterprises, but more as a Tzotzil-speaking collectivity than as individual citizens of Mexico or the world.

Through his close, careful, and critical attention to the mango, the chile pepper, and the truck, Alvarez offers us an insightful and indispensable view of how transnationalism plays itself out on the ground in contemporary Mexico. He shows how the economic and political power that seems grounded at the border actually extends hundreds and thousands of miles beyond it. He reveals how the culturally based logic of *la maroma* enables Mexican *chileros* to participate and sometimes prosper in the lucrative U.S. market. He demonstrates how transnational trade has transformed interregional relations in Mexico, producing a new cognitive mapping of the nation and its people.

By going "beyond the border" Alvarez teaches us to look for the unanticipated, unexpected, and even unlikely consequences of transnationalism. His work shows us as well that we cannot look at the border from only one direction. Transnational trade has changed Mexico, but it has changed the United States as well. In his discussions of the meaning of Mexican-American identity in the practical business activities of Los Angeles fruit and vegetable markets and in the self-imaginings of an older generation of Mexican-Americans, Alvarez deftly delineates the dialectical and mutually constitutive qualities of social structure and culture.

Alvarez examines how social practices and social institutions produce identities and give them their determinate social meaning. Mexican-American and Chicano identities in the United States have a long history rooted in external negative ascription and social exclusion on the one hand, but in internal positive affirmation and community making on the other hand. When it comes to long-standing historical grievances, nothing from the past ever disappears completely; the identities of aggrieved racialized groups are perpetually shaped by the unresolved legacies of past injustices. The past, however, never fully explains the present. Identities are not merely inherited from the past, they are dynamically re-created every day under socially and historically specific circumstances. Alvarez augments our understanding of these dynamics powerfully by identifying the institutions, practices, experiences, and ideas that shape the subjectivities of the *mexicanos* that form the focal point of his studies.

In the United States, race relations are always property relations. "Raced" people are not just devalued psychically and spiritually by prejudice and discrimination, they also face systematic impediments to accumulating assets, making investments, and bargaining over wages and working conditions. But they are not helpless. Rather, people of color in the United States have become experts at turning "segregation into congregation," at turning common experiences with discrimination and exclusion into elaborate networks of mutuality and solidarity.[3]

Mexican-origin entrepreneurs in the Los Angeles markets utilize their proximity to Mexico and the knowledge of distribution channels in that country to secure desired products on favorable terms. They compensate for their exclusion from other sectors of the economy by contacting new immigrants and turning them into their customers and their employees. Victimized by hierarchies outside the market, they benefit from an internal hierarchy that leaves newcomers with the least desirable jobs but gives certain advantages and opportunities to U.S. citizens and longtime residents. It is not simply that these entrepreneurs avail themselves of the opportunities offered them because of the ethnic/national/racial identity they share with new immigrants, but more interestingly that business needs themselves generate an ethnic identity based on reciprocal obligations and responsibilities.

Similarly, in his evocative, reflective, and moving analysis of later life identifications with *mexicanidad* by Mexican-Americans from Lemon Grove, California, who have lived most or all of their lives in the United States, Alvarez challenges the ethnicity model and its predictions of gradual assimilation through ethnic deracination. The people Alvarez studies succeed in business, participate in politics, and display complete command of the English language. Yet they maintain ties with their ancestors' communities, disidentify with the United States, and choose to speak in Spanish or interlingually. Alvarez explains these contradictions as the product of the "deep territorialization" of the border, of the sense of specific belonging that living near the border transmits to the residents of Lemon Grove. Their later-life reidentification with Mexico is a way of speaking back to all of the insults they encountered over the years on the U.S. side of the border, against the teachers and bosses who required them to speak English and Anglicize their names, against the newspapers, motion pictures, and advertising imagery that have systematically defamed them and their culture, even against the Mexican voices who scolded them for being *too* "American" and not Mexican enough. Caught in between conflicting imperatives for most of their lives, in their later years they deploy their cultural knowledge, tastes, and preferences to slip into an identity that feels comfortable, that makes them feel at home.

The border is not simply a line between nations; it is a nexus of power with social ramifications and consequences thousands of miles away. It is not a boundary, nor is a boundary really wanted by a bounded nation like the United States that is committed to the pursuit of boundless markets. The border is a generator of inequality, a device where profits can be made by playing off one group of workers against another. Crossing the border without documentation can have brutal consequences for desperate low-wage workers, but crossing the border is a major project of capital and the state. Once we go "beyond the border" as Alvarez asks us to do, we see that the power of the border may well be strongest where it is least evident.

As San Diego resident and "taco shop poet" Adrian Arancibia asks at the conclusion of his poem "La Línea":

> will we ever really cross the line
> or will we just sit
> encumbered
> by the borders of our own minds[4]

Introduction

This book grows out of events in my own life. While I was growing up, the fruit and vegetable trade was important to my family, as was the U.S.–Mexico border. Both the border and the "markets" (a familiar term) were interwoven into the daily lives of the people I knew. As a young man, I strove to succeed in the market environment, but in college and graduate school I sought a deeper realization of the experiences of my family and community. As an anthropologist, I initially reconstructed my family's migration into the United States, then committed myself to the application of the discipline and dedicated my efforts to a variety of practical research venues. Little did I know when I ventured into the anthropological that I would return to the life of the markets and the U.S.–Mexico border. This eventual return was a dramatic syncopation in my career as an anthropologist. In 1984, I found myself in a political-economic quagmire and sought refuge in the trade I knew best, returning to work alongside my father, Robert O. Alvarez Castellanos, in the produce trade.

I grew up in San Diego and spent crucial periods of my youth in the market environment. I now realize that the fruit and vegetable business was a central part of my socialization. From a very early age, I was trained by my father in the trade. As I grew up, I worked at various times in the family "store" learning the basics of handling merchandise and the necessary tools of the produce business. I learned to drive backing large bobtail trucks in the produce yard, and my first venture on the road (at fifteen and unlicensed) was behind the wheel of a two-ton stake bed loaded to the hilt.

Most of my early acquaintances stemmed from these experiences, and I grew to learn that the "markets" were central to many of my kin. Indeed, San Diego's Sixth Street Produce Market, like all such markets, was a kinship of its own. Produce row was steeped in ethnicity and contrasted sharply with the type of color line in my high school (brown and Anglo) and in the neighborhoods of San Diego, which during the 1950s were still very segregated. Chinese, Italian, Jew, Mexican, Greek, Japanese, black, and others mixed into the reality of the market. Competition was keen, but as I remember it now there existed a certain codependency, resolve, and tolerance among vendors. A certain trust was etched with the risks of the marketplace. These experiences ingrained a specific sentiment and realization of the market life, of produce, truckers, and entrepreneurs, which emerge in my interpretive work on global markets and distribution. Like the produce entrepreneurs I describe, the produce activity "got in my blood."

My college years (1961–66) were focused on a newfound interest—anthropology—but summers and vacations I spent at the markets in San Diego working for college tuition. A three-and-a-half-year stint in the U.S. Peace Corps after college impressed on me the value of culturally and socially informed programs of change, and although I vowed to enter graduate school, I again returned to the Sixth Street Market. The pull of the market, the kinship, and the familial obligation nurtured through the better part of my life brought me back. When I left the markets for graduate school, I believed it was for good.

The politically conservative Reagan era of the 1980s brought relentless cutbacks and the termination of social and educational programs. The educational programs I worked in were not only ended but ruthlessly dismantled. In 1984, this time armed with the tools of anthropology, I made my way back to the produce rows of the Los Angeles Wholesale Terminal (LAWT) and reentered the family business. For the next five years I worked in a variety of settings in the wholesale fruit and vegetable trade, first in the Los Angeles Wholesale Terminal, then in Mexico in Tijuana, Baja California, and (the year before entering an academic life) San Luis Río Colorado. The trade and product I worked with was principally Mexican. Alongside other Mexican entrepreneurs I became vested as a *chilero*, a chile specialist. I initially worked out of a chile packing shed in Tijuana as the principal vendor of fresh chile and coconuts to the LAWT. As part of this effort I ventured into the chile production areas of coastal and central Mexico, and then the mango fields of Sinaloa, Nayarit, Jalisco, and Michoacán in an effort to learn this trade and the requirements of export shipping. In 1988–89, I worked with Mexican farmers supervising and overseeing the production and packing of broccoli and green onions from Sonora and the Mexicali Valley. These ventures took me into the interior of Mexico sourcing fruit, visiting markets and entrepreneurs, and connecting to the distributors in Los Angeles across the U.S.–Mexican line.

During this period, I crossed the border daily and learned the intricacies of border personnel and truck crossings. As anthropologist-ethnographer I wrote copious notes and market information in notebooks I carried everywhere (being branded "él del cuaderno," he of the notebook, by friends in the trade). These experiences enhanced and nurtured my anthropological perspective of a greater sociological context conditioned by global economies and the geopolitical border of the nation-state—a long way of saying that these specific experiences and histories conditioned my interpretation of the border and the global process reported in this book.

As I moved through the various scenarios of market entrepreneurial activity, in both Mexico and the United States, I realized that the people of "the markets" are intimately tied to one another. The farmer or market vendor in Jalisco was attuned to the pulses of economic activity in the northern frontier and often to the Los Angeles Wholesale Terminal. Talk of the market quickly focused on entrepreneurial possibilities. Individuals relied on and strategically utilized experience and knowledge of investment, banking, and cultural capital that was tied to specific products and consumers. The border, which hindered the crossing of both trucks and products, became a variable in the competition of marketing. Yet in this simple equation I learned to see the influence of the large U.S. distributors and the U.S. nation-state in production regions. I also learned that for both U.S. and Mexican entrepreneurs this social-economic web is a known entity in which they must work.

The specific instances of transnational behavior I write about here are tied to a broad web of interaction, economics, and information flow. The sale of tropical fruits in Los Angeles is intimately tied not only to U.S. distributors and Mexican producers but to the entrepreneurs and transporters who are engaged in the trade, as well as the immigrant consumers who buy and have created these new "ethnic markets." This context is contained and often nurtured by the action of the nation-state itself. Fostered by nation-state boundary (border) control and security, the dynamics of fruit and vegetable distribution beyond the border, I argue, are ultimately controlled by institutionally produced state sanctions.

The U.S.–Mexico border is crucial in this social landscape but was somewhat of an anomaly in the early stages of my life. Both crucial and vivid as a regulator of life instances, it was also a backdrop that evaded resolution. The border was a constant, like the air and geography that pervaded the community of extended kin and friends of which I was lucky to be a part. The border was just there: in the presence of elders and in the continual visits of cousins, aunts, and uncles who came from Tijuana, Ensenada, and Tecate to be with us on various occasions. When I was young, my family crossed the border into the *colonias* of Tijuana where kin resided. Later, I discovered the lure of Coahuila and the nightlife that drew us as teenagers into adventures now legendary in our repertoires of border crossings. The sights and sounds of the border are mixed with baptisms, Our Lady of Guadalupe in Logan Heights, North Avenue and Olive Streets in Lemon Grove, events shared with my grandfather and uncles, my grandmother in her rocker, meals in the restaurants of Tijuana, and memories of early ventures into the heart of my family's past. The scenarios of my youth are mixed with a specific border defined by the cultural resonance of our daily lives. This also included a certain dissonance of life as a Chicano in the United States, formed by the pervasiveness of discrimination and hierarchical under-pinnings in San Diego. Yet this evasive border, as place, has specific meaning bound to the history and the events of people's lives. This reality was illuminated in my return as an anthropologist.

In 1984 I began crossing the border as a *chilero* and market entrepreneur and learned to see the U.S.–Mexico border in a more precise manner. The specificity of border custom, border people (especially controlling personnel), and border social behavior stood out in vivid contrast to the seemingly casual crossings of my earlier experiences and those of family immigrants who crossed into the United States prior to the bureaucratization of the border. Enhanced by the competitive nature of the produce trade and its perishable commodity of fruits and vegetables, the border and its hierarchical complexity took on new meaning. I began to see the contemporary border "from the other side": through Mexican eyes. Truck crossings, for example, entailed not only the customs screening in the United States but a complex set of personnel on the Mexican side, where fruit was processed and prepared specifically for the U.S. market. Mexican brokers and officials sanctioned crossings, while bank and commercial entities recorded export value. The markets of Tijuana buzzed with activity as small and large entrepreneurs rushed to make commercial border closings and ensure the delivery of orders placed by distributors in Los Angeles. The border syncopated life for the communities of market personnel and common laborers who were tied to the cultural and economic patterns of the chile and ethnic produce trade. The participation and engagement in the trade fostered the interpretations presented here of the markets, the social organization of *fruteros*, and the broader institutional structures embedded in border control. Such complexity informed and helped me interrogate the broader meaning of border crossing, control, and nation-state prerogatives.

Needless to say, the perspective of the people who engage the border and the activities presented here is key to understanding the transnational nature of this border activity. The ethnographic profiles presented in this book are based on ground-up views of a broader economic and social process. They represent the logical sense of people engaged in the trade and border movement, but are textured in the larger social fields of social-cultural interpretation. My own involvement in these activities was based on earning a living, and I engaged the business and social matrix with vigor. My anthropological training helped me unravel the socioeconomic processes in which I was involved. Although I had grown up in the trade, I learned new methods and how to do this work in Mexico, on the border. The individuals I worked with taught me well, and I left the market life a richer person. The *troqueros*, loaders, other *fruteros*, and the many workers we relied on to get product to market are crucial in the ethnographic portraits, as well as in the interpretations I present here. I am not only grateful to them all but take great pride in having worked alongside them. These folk are often left out of the equations of the transnational and global, yet they make up the rudimentary foundations of these processes. The packers and sorters of chile pepper bound for the L.A. market may never venture across the border, but they are key players in transnational U.S.–Mexican trade. The essence of these experiences and their meaning is part of the contemporary social context of transnational and global behavior. They entail everyday experience and the recognition that people are not only aware of their immediate social-economic circumstances but act strategically in their engagement of the transnational.

This work would not have been possible without the assistance of many friends and relatives. Most important is my father, Roberto Alvarez Castellanos, who not only engaged me in the produce markets on both sides of the U.S.–Mexico border but provided me with the opportunity to experience a Mexico I had never known. I also want to thank the numerous people of the trade I worked with, many of whom were true mentors. José Cabrera López and Jay Nelson were true *compañeros* during a very difficult time. The book would not have been possible without the assistance, editorial guidance, and creative ideas of George Lipsitz and the initial help of Charles Briggs. I thank the journal *Human Organizations* for permission to reprint chapters 1 and 2; George A. Collier and the *American Ethnologist* for permission to reprint chapter 3; and the

Journal of the West for permission to reprint chapter 5. George A. Collier, John Chance, James Greenberg, Robert Hackenberg, and Tomás Weaver provided critical comments for these and other essays. Dwight Wheeler and Anne Goldberg contributed valuable research assistance in the preparation of chapters 1 and 2.

The ethnographic experiences reported here were important periods of my life, which my family shared and lived with me. To them, especially to Karen Annie, I owe thanks for their patience and understanding.

Many people contributed to this book, but I alone am responsible for any errors of fact.

CHAPTER 1

Beyond the Border:
El Mango in Global Perspective

Three decades ago, people in the United States rarely consumed mangos. Today, the United States is the leading mango-importing nation in the world. More than a matter of mere change in consumer taste, the dramatic growth of mango consumption in the United States offers an illustrative example of the ways in which new patterns of transnational trade, migration, and investment are altering national identities and institutions.

The same processes that have made the United States the world's leading mango importer have made Mexico the world's largest mango exporter. The accelerated movement of mangos across the U.S.–Mexico border changes economic, social, cultural, and political practices in both nations. It also has effects far away, in the entire American hemisphere, in Africa, and in Asia. It enables us to see how an alteration in something that seems so simple—the identity of produce on supermarket shelves—might be part and parcel of a broader transformation that is changing the nature of social membership and citizenship everywhere in the world.

As people and products move across borders at ever-accelerating rates, the texture and tone of contemporary commerce and culture are increasingly defined by transnational institutions, activities, and investments. The nation-state and its agents, however, do not disappear during transnational times. Indeed, they become more important than ever.

As part of free-trade agreements, the U.S. Department of Agriculture (USDA) regulates entry of fruits and vegetables into the United States. Regulation takes place purportedly because of the high susceptibility of specific fruits such as the mango to dangerous pests that might threaten U.S. production and markets. Green, nonhusked coconuts, sugarcane, Mexican plums, and other tropical varieties are prohibited because of the dangers to U.S. agriculture of fruit-fly contamination. But threats to U.S. markets are also a consideration, as in the case of avocados, where the principles of free trade succumb to the power of local interests (Stanford 1998).

Mangos are not allowed into the United States in their natural state. Yet geometrically increasing import demands and a geometrically multiplying market for mangos forced the USDA to implement sanitation processes, under strict guidelines, to allow U.S. distributors to import the fruit. These policies greatly assist efforts by agribusiness firms to control mango production in Mexico, while at the same time extending the domain and power of a U.S. government agency far into the hinterlands of Mexico.

The USDA and the U.S. Customs Service regulate the flow of fruit and vegetables entering the United States at specific ports of entry, but such control also extends into agricultural production regions. At the border, USDA officials randomly screen agricultural products, such as chile, for pesticide content. Chile exceeding tolerable U.S. Environmental Protection Agency pesticide levels is denied entry. This results in the quarantine of production regions and the prohibition against their shipping to U.S. ports of entry. Shipping and border crossing resumes only when pesticide application in interior sites of production is corrected, documented, and certified by the USDA. Such regulation by the U.S. nation-state beyond the border exerts a profound influence on offshore production, markets, and distribution. As the North American Free Trade Agreement (NAFTA) expands, such regulatory control will not only continue, but will also reach into new arenas.

The influence and control of the U.S nation-state on offshore mango production and distribution takes place largely through the activities of the USDA's Animal and Plant Health Inspection Service (USDA-APHIS). The regulation and control of the Mexican mango market trade by the USDA illustrates how NAFTA works indirectly to promote the expansion of U.S. interests throughout the hemisphere.

The activities of the USDA extend far beyond the geographic point that is the border. The agency has not only entered the Mexican nation-state, it has also encroached upon all areas of the hemisphere where mangos are produced for export to the United States. This is both fascinating and distressing when we think of the influence the USDA, a U.S. nation-state agency, exerts in places far beyond national borders. My concern lies not only in the extensive presence of the United States throughout the hemisphere, but also in its role in the larger processes of globalism, its influence in the hierarchical control of market economies, labor, and its effects on people at local levels of production and distribution. What might appear to be agreements facilitating "free" trade between equals in reality become mechanisms for ensuring dominance by U.S. firms over domestic markets and overseas sources of raw materials.[1]

The U.S.–Mexico border has long been a site of marked transnational and global processes, as well as the site marking the divide between two nation-states. The current scholarly and political focus on borders, and in particular the U.S.–Mexico border, has helped flesh out the nuances and particularities of human activity involved in transnationalism. In this manifestation of globalism, the local-level behavior of people illustrates a complex reordering of identities, economies, and political persuasions.

The nation-state manages transnationalism. It deploys agents at points of entry to control the movements of commodities and humans. The nation-state establishes policies about labor–management relations, taxation, environmental regulation, and policing that produce economic incentives or disincentives for border crossings. It establishes standards, terms, and conditions on importation and immigration that influence activities thousands of miles away from the border itself, deep inside the territory of both sending and receiving nations.

The U.S. Immigration and Naturalization Service (INS) and its

Border Patrol, for example, extend the border to checkpoints and regions of surveillance north of the geopolitical line—along highways in Arizona, inside high schools in Nebraska, at meatpacking plants in Minnesota, and on construction sites in New York. The Border Patrol's territory increasingly extends beyond the "border" as raids on places of employment and sweeps through ethnic neighborhoods take place in cities throughout the United States. Such control often disregards the civil rights of citizens, as in 1996 when the INS and city police in Chandler, Arizona (a hundred miles north of the border), questioned, rounded up, and detained hundreds of people solely on the basis of Latino phenotypic features, turning all U.S. Latinos into suspected border violators (Schaus 2000).

Mangos and other newly marketed ethnic products are part of a historical matrix that involves Latino immigration into the United States, the creation of transnational markets, efforts to increase the supply of low-wage labor and ensure its profitable exploitation, and current patterns of production and distribution. The movement of immigrants into the United States is a part of a labor market expansion, which includes new patterns of settlement and a resulting demand for new products (see Alvarez 1991, 1994, 1995). Chile and mangos, along with other ethnic products, have become central to the growth and development of major U.S. transnational distributors and producers. The increase of ethnic immigrants (the implosion of the third world into the first) and the growth of indigenous U.S. minorities have generated new market developments over the last two decades. These activities have propelled the growth of multimillion dollar businesses focusing on the ethnic trade.

The role of the USDA appears benign when controlling possibly dangerous threats to U.S. agricultural production. But it appears less benign when influencing the market activity of U.S. distributors and wholesalers of specific fruit varieties.

Immigrant demand for special foods from home countries has grown spectacularly in large U.S. urban centers. For example, half of all mangos exported from Mexico to the United States are consumed in Los Angeles, a city where an estimated 50 percent of new Mexican immigrants reside alongside many people from other mango-consuming nations (U.S. Bureau of the Census 2005). In a country where only one-third of all Euro American homes have ever purchased the fruit, it becomes apparent that ethnic newcomers from Asia, Africa, the Caribbean, and Central and South America are the major consumers of the new tropical fruit varieties. Yet it is not enough to state that migrants create the demand for such ethnic products.

The immigrant tide (and the resulting demand for specific commodities) is part of a hemispheric shift that is intimately connected to labor needs in the United States. From this perspective, mangos and other ethnic fruit items are not free-flowing commodities controlled simply by market demand. Demand is but one part of a greater sociological matrix, hierarchically ordered, at the top of which is the nation-state. The rise of hemispheric systems, represented in part by nation-state agreements such as NAFTA, are tied to immigration, redefinitions of the functional maps of "national" territories, technological advances, and market behavior. This is the other side of NAFTA, wherein state prerogatives are revealed. These broader systems have enormous effects at local levels, on people as well as on production. What I call *El Mango*, the Mexican mango trade, and in particular the export/import trade between Mexico and the United States, illustrates these dynamics clearly.

El Mango is a hemispheric system controlled by the United States through transnational businesses and nation-state agencies. *El Mango* encompasses activities in the territory beyond the literal U.S.–Mexico border, in all the orchards, packing sheds, and offices where laborers, middlemen, and transnational corporate executives negotiate labor relations, nation-state prerogatives, the needs of capital, and the emergence of specific technologies to define the mango trade.

It is no simple irony that Mexico, the United States' nearest neighbor to the south and source of its largest immigrant population, is the world's largest exporter of mangos, or that the United States, a country where mangos were rarely seen until a couple of decades ago, is now the world's largest importer. These population–product links are not solely the result of immigrant demand and market supply. They have their roots in the expansion of capital supported by political interests in the hemisphere. The encroachment of the U.S. nation-state into political arenas inducting immigration beyond its borders is well documented (see, for example, Dosal 1993; Langley and Schoonover 1995). Similarly, the role of the United States in the control of export commodities underlies the dynamics of transnational trade.

Like other writers (Stanford 1994; Wells 1996; McMichael 1995), I view the Mexican mango industry as a system, a vertically integrated commodity chain. My emphasis, however, is on the hierarchical tendencies defined by power, vested not only in capital vis-à-vis transnational corporations and finance, but also in border control and its extension by the nation-state. The nation-state and its agencies not only support U.S. transnationals but create specific hierarchies to which people in areas beyond the borders are forced to respond. Successful markets depend on capital expansion and continued control of vast territory and thus labor, of infrastructure and social organization.

My argument is based on both research and participation in the trade from 1986 through 1988, and on tours in Sinaloa and Nayarit in 1994 and 1998. From 1986 to the present, *El Mango* has undergone profound changes. Like other ethnic products such as chile, mangos are linked to new immigrant populations in the United States (Alvarez 1995; Kainuma 1997). Mangos are most popular in cities with large Latino and Asian populations (*RAP Market Information* 2002). Consumption of fresh mangos per capita in the United States rose 216 percent in the decade 1986–95 (Kainuma 1997, 27). In 1995–96 alone, U.S. consumption grew by 15 percent (ibid., 28).

El Mango offers an exemplary illustration of the dynamic links and transformations that characterize transnationalism. Asia produces approximately 75 percent of the world's mangos (12 million metric tons). Ninety percent of that production takes place in India, China, Pakistan, Thailand, and Indonesia. After Asia, North and Central America and Africa follow with 10 percent of world production in each region (Kainuma 1997, 18). India, the world's largest producer, has been growing mangos for more than four thousand years.

Mangos entered the Western Hemisphere as a colonial import that spread rapidly. The Portuguese brought the mango to Brazil around 1700, and it made its way to Mexico from the Philippines around 1775 (ibid., 17, 48). Today, mangos are the world's second-most frequently produced tropical fruit, trailing only bananas (ibid., 18). Out of the total world production of 418,877,800 pounds (19 million metric tons) in 1995, India produced some 220,462,000 pounds (10 million metric tons) of mangos annually, making it first in world production.

Mangos have become Mexico's most valuable agricultural export commodity. Surprisingly, Mexico, with only 2,954,000 pounds (1.34 million metric tons), is second in annual world production. Mexico's production, however, amounts to about two-thirds of all mangos produced in the hemisphere (ibid., 20). Although Mexico exports more fresh mangos than any other nation (the Philippines is second), this represents only 10 percent of total Mexican production. The remaining 90 percent is consumed in Mexico. This raises important questions concerning the role of Mexico as a peripheral supplier to the United States (see Alvarez 1994 for a similar discussion on the chile export market). In 1995, Mexico exported 290,385 pounds of mangos to the United States, bringing in U.S. $105 million (Tropical Produce Marketing News 1996). The United States imports 65–85 percent of its mangos from Mexico, accounting for 85 percent of Mexico's export crop. The remainder comes primarily from Haiti, or is grown in Puerto Rico and Florida (USDA Marketing Service 1997; Empacadoras de Mango de Exportación 2003).

Between 1986 and 1996, the global export mango trade grew exponentially, with the United States as the primary importer. In this ten-year period, total world export increased 64 percent (Kainuma 1997, 20) while Mexican exports tripled (Tropical Produce Marketing News 1996). In the past three decades, the export trade to the United States has grown an incredible 4,500 percent. In 1967–68, 142,000 pounds of mangos crossed into the country at Nogales, Arizona. By 1997, this had increased to a whopping 312,550,000 pounds (153,160,000 pounds at Nogales, with an additional 159,390,000 pounds crossing into South Texas) (USDA Marketing Report 1997).

Mangos are grown throughout Mexico's southern states, but the export crop is limited to the Pacific West and follows a seasonal cycle beginning in February and ending in late August or early September. *El Mango* encompasses the western Pacific states of Chiapas, Oaxaca, Guerrero, Michoacán, Colima, Jalisco, Nayarit, and Sinaloa. Mangos from Central and South America enter the United States in the Mexican off-season—October through March. This makes mangos available in the United States all year because Mexico and the southern regions have been pulled into hemispheric trade and competition.

The two principal varieties of mangos grown in Mexico and throughout the Southern Hemisphere are the Manila and Florida types. Tommy Atkins, Haden, and Kent are the primary export varieties originally developed in Florida. Since the mid-1990s, the Manila Altaufo (primarily from Chiapas) has also been exported with great market success. The production of *El Mango* is tied to varieties initially introduced and controlled by U.S. interests and incorporates vast numbers of people in production, harvest labor, packing, transportation, and marketing.

U.S. certification of *El Mango* proceeds through strict controls demanding complex technologies and large amounts of capital. The regulation of the mango trade is linked to the product's susceptibility to a number of varieties of the fruit fly. This pest is among the most feared in commercial agriculture. The logic of control is that any contamination by the fruit fly has the potential to destroy major U.S. agricultural production, and subsequently marketing systems on which American farmers, distributors, and consumers depend.

There is no denying the danger of fruit-fly exposure, but the extent to which such regulation is aimed at market control and influence in Mexico and other exporting nations in the Western Hemisphere warrants careful examination. The implementation of this control is almost exclusively based on U.S. prerogatives. Mangos destined for Canada, for example, are not required to be processed according to current USDA standards.

Mango production at the local level throughout the Mexican republic is processed in mango packing sheds (*empacadoras*) where U.S.

certification occurs. *Empacadora* owners and managers control labor and orchards and confront the daily problems associated with a complex array of activities that are exacerbated by the stringent demands of U.S. certification. Some of these packing-shed operators are growers, but the majority are middlemen who buy and sell mangos to U.S. distributors. In fact, a new breed of *manguero* (mango fruit entrepreneur) is surfacing. Professionals with training in law, architecture, and other backgrounds now enter the trade, and young, newly trained *ingenieros agrónomos* (agronomists) are being recruited into *El Mango*.

Mango export depends on access to U.S. markets, usually through connections with U.S.-based distributors. A variety of contract relations are possible with American firms. Some U.S. distributors form partnerships with specific *empacadoras* that enable them to secure all the fruit packed and processed by that particular plant, thereby assuring continuous supply of the product for markets in major U.S. cities. Such partnerships involve capital outlay for construction, machinery, and operations, as in other Mexican export markets (Alvarez 1994). In addition to partnerships, contracts can include simply buying processed fruit through established relationships whereby packing sheds promise certain amounts (and quality) of fruit to U.S. distributors. There are many variations in these two primary types of contracts.

The business activities that structure relations between *empacadoras* and mango buyers (distributors) have become more complex since the introduction of the present system of U.S. mango certification. Although seemingly straightforward and scientifically designed, certification induced a variety of strategies and responses in local areas.

Prior to 1987, ethylene dibromide fumigation served as the primary treatment for mangos destined for U.S. markets (United States Department of Agriculture-APHIS 1990). In that year, the U.S. Environmental Protection Agency banned the use of ethylene dibromide, triggering a new system of treatment for mangos and other tropical fruits susceptible to the fruit fly. The ethylene dibromide fumigation was a relatively simple process for fumigating mangos in closed chambers after packing. USDA officers stationed at Mexican packing plants watched over the processing of mangos destined for the U.S. market. Once fumigation was completed, these officials manually sealed trailers loaded with mangos, which then headed for their destination in the United States.

At the border, USDA officials reviewed certification and had the option to sample truck lots randomly for possible fruit-fly infestation. Any signs of the fruit fly destined a truckload to return to Mexico. Similarly, loads with tampered USDA seals were also rejected. Oddly, this control invested U.S. officials in Mexico with full authority to control mango loads and oversee specific packing shed activities tied to export. In recent years, U.S. control and presence has grown and become even stricter.

Initially, U.S. inspectors spent sixty-day intervals at packing sheds with all expenses paid by the packers. A large deposit of fifteen to twenty thousand dollars funded salaries based on eight-hour days, overtime pay, travel, room and board, and other expenses for uniformed officials, who often lived on-site. As the mango exports grew, however, so too did the responsibilities of U.S. officials in the mango regions.

The USDA developed the hot-water immersion system in 1987 and provided Mexican *mangueros* access to a few of its manufacturers, as well as to the specific plans and specifications of the new treatment (United States Department of Agriculture-APHIS 1990, 1993a, 1993b, 1993c, 1994a, 1994b). The USDA subsequently approved a hot-air treatment as a substitute, but the expense involved in this process prohibits current use in Mexico. Under the new requirements, all unpacked fruit had to be submerged at least four inches in a hot-water bath of 115 degrees for ninety minutes. Water temperature could not drop below 113.8 degrees Fahrenheit, and the aggregate time that the water needed to fall between 113.8 and 114.8 degrees was not to exceed fifteen minutes, although approval was based on ten minutes.

By October 1987, all export states in Mexico, except Chiapas— where fruit-fly infestation was strong—had secured approval from the USDA for hot-water treatment. Since then, Chiapas has been added to the approved list, and a few changes to this basic procedure have been made. Initially, in 1988, processed fruit frequently had very poor appearance and a short shelf life. As a consequence, the time in water was reduced to seventy-five minutes for smaller varieties, and other postharvest and posttreatment procedures, such as immediate refrigeration and cooling tanks, were introduced at the sheds themselves.

This process required a complex set of engineering protocols. The USDA provided specifications and a checklist for minimum requirements, but no construction plans. *Mangueros* were left the task of developing the machinery and designs to meet USDA specifications, including the design of packing sheds and the engineering specifications of the hot-water treatment facilities. Initially, USDA inspection and certification focused solely on the hot-water system, but later involved the entire contents of the packing shed, including electrical and electronic components, computers and microprocessors, climate-controlled rooms, surge protectors, electrical generators (recommended), boilers and thermostatic controls, temperature sensors, continuous water circulation, temperature recorders, alarm systems, insect-free enclosures, cooling tanks, and specific safety and health requirements (e.g., hard hats).

In addition, certification requires a work plan signed by representatives of each shed, by the host government's department of agriculture, and by the USDA-APHIS. Thus, the USDA first inspected and approved all plans for packing sheds as well as for the actual treatment machinery. Once plans were approved and construction was under way, USDA agents made preliminary inspections and offered recommendations about needed changes. When the entire plant was ready, a test of the treatment facility took place. Hence, *mangueros* were absolutely subject to USDA requirements for their participation in the export trade. Currently, once *empacadoras* pass all requirements for the treatment of the fruit, they are certified for the season. Each year, the packing shed must be recertified. The recertification process costs between fifteen and twenty thousand dollars, once the packing sheds are fully equipped and ready for inspection.

In 1988, thirty-three Mexican packing-shed companies requested certification by the USDA. Initially, one individual who had been the head of a major national export association won the concession in Mexico to build an approved prototype that was eventually sold to existing exporters. The prototype was *el túnel*, a thirty-meter immersion tank. This involved a massive conveyor-belt system passing mangos through the hot-water tunnel for ninety minutes. *El túnel* became the prototype produced on a large scale in the mango region. The cost of each system was about sixty thousand dollars, but in 1988 the peso collapse sent shock waves through the mango world. In addition to poor marketability for the treated mango entering the United States, the high costs of *el túnel* caused a downturn in the export business.

Dependence on *el túnel* ended when *mangueros* began constructing their own systems. Today, each *empacadora* designs and constructs its own tanks following the basic specifications, requirements, and recommendations of the USDA. Empacadoras send plans to USDA offices in the United States, where they are reviewed and approved. Periodic construction checks by the USDA include supervision and suggestions about packing-shed design and construction.

The growth in the numbers of mango exporters placed further responsibility on the USDA to complete certification. The thirty-three *empacadoras* in 1988 grew to seventy-four in 1997 (Kainuma 1997, 54). The USDA increased its inspections, but U.S. officials in Mexico soon found themselves overextended. In an effort to maintain certification standards, the USDA decided to deputize Mexican nationals as USDA inspection officers.

Eventually, the USDA formally relinquished its continuous on-site inspections of the packing sheds and placed the surveillance of the hot-water treatment in the hands of Empacadoras de Mango de Exportación (EMEX), a privatized Mexican institution. Today, EMEX conducts on-site supervision and provides Mexican inspectors for the export trade. The final control of certification, however, continues to lie with the USDA-APHIS.

In literature distributed by the USDA and EMEX, certification is the responsibility of this Mexican entity, but the USDA continues to be identified by *mangueros* as the institution in control. All certification and approval comes from the U.S. agency. It is clear to everyone involved that EMEX is only an affiliate that provides inspectors. The deputizing of national inspectors, and then the allocation of this activity to EMEX, was a way for the USDA to resolve its limited manpower resources for continued on-site control over the treatment and export of *El Mango*.

The USDA has deputized inspectors in all regions from which mangos are exported to the United States, not only in Mexico. The nation-state thereby reaches offshore into faraway production regions that include Brazil, Peru, Ecuador, Nicaragua, Guatemala, Haiti, and the Dominican Republic. This extended control raises serious questions concerning nation-state encroachment, the extension of border sanctions, and the influence of nation-state institutions and their representatives on hemispheric trade.

The growth of mango exports from Mexico parallels the dynamics of other global changes and technological advances. Packing sheds now feature the latest computers provided by Honeywell and Conti (for tracking mango treatment), high-tech sensors, and alarm systems. Sophisticated technical procedures have been absorbed by *mangueros* in their daily activities, revolutionizing the trade within Mexico and adding to the dramatically increased volume of fruit exported into the United States.

The improvement of infrastructure and communication has been dramatic. Communication in the past relied on telephone systems that were often unreliable or unavailable in distant rural areas. Communication with truckers and middlemen throughout the mango region was slow and often difficult. Today, Mexican *mangueros* use cell phones that allow them access not only to timely information about markets and fruit transport and arrival, but also about regional activity and competition in the trade. This innovation has liberated the *mangueros* and other fruit specialists who were once tied to specific mango territories. Now, a *manguero* stands in a remote field in Nayarit and communicates with Mexico City and Guadalajara to learn about local activity, calls U.S. brokers to check on fruit and current market prices while selling and sourcing fruit for shipment, and makes calls to packing sheds to give shipment orders and to make daily arrangements concerning procedure and management. One young *chilero-manguero* I met in a restaurant in Sinaloa responded, within the space of an hour, to a dozen calls concerning the export trade and other business.

The cell phone has made the entire mango region accessible to exporters. The new professional *manguero* is attuned to production and processing activities across an unbounded set of transnational production sites. The enterprise has become globalized. Differences in labor contracts, labor organization, and gender preferences for workers are compared across regions, and the nuances of producers and packers in specific areas concerning access and sourcing of fruit are well known elsewhere. Improved roads and other technologies enhance trade and make interregional control and access possible.

Although the certification process is rigidly structured and *mangueros* must adhere to scientific and engineering specifications in building facilities and processing mangos, local-level behavior illustrates interesting accommodations aimed at gaining strategic advantages in marketing. In Mexico, the inspectors and certification officers are viewed by most *mangueros* as an imposed but necessary evil. Most *mangueros* attempt to cultivate favorable relationships with inspectors to influence decisions about peripheral activities related to production. Inspectors have the authority to close sheds and reject loads because of unsanitary conditions. The action they take on unsanitary conditions can mean losing at least a full day's processing and packing. Good relations with inspectors may lead to more leniency in allowing the shed to clear decayed fruit and continue with packing. Losing a day of packing could represent the withholding of several loads of mangos, each worth up to forty thousand dollars in strong markets.

Empacadoras consequently cultivate goodwill with inspectors, meeting their every demand. Inspectors are driven to and from hotels, fed at restaurants, provided with rental cars, and invited to *manguero* homes. The actual process of certification cannot be tampered with, but the attitudes of inspectors and their decisions about nontreatment requirements leave room for judgment and offer possible advantages. *Mangueros* feel that the process is necessary, but that the interpretation of the rules is too strict. "Los gringos son muy exagerados" (The gringos are too exaggerated), said one *manguero*. "If they find one infested mango, they'll reject entire loads," said another.

Transnational production, distribution, and marketing are increasingly complex processes. U.S. certification of *El Mango* encompasses a rigid technology requiring high capital investment and subsequent hierarchical ordering of the production, processing, and exporting of mangos to the United States. The role of the USDA in the mango market and its influence on both U.S. and Mexican *mangueros*, packing sheds, and labor are tied to broader initiatives.

The expansion of this trade into Central and South America is heavily influenced by the parameters of U.S. certification and raises issues concerning NAFTA and trade in general. How does this broad imperative influence the control and organization of labor in the fields and in the packing sheds? To what extent does certification influence Mexican *mangueros* in forming contractual relations with large U.S. distributors?

These are issues tied to hemispheric initiatives (such as NAFTA) and to emerging postcolonial and postindustrial processes. They are defined by nation-state prerogatives that take shape within a global marketplace and current global dynamics. Capital, finance, and transnational businesses dominate this equation, but the incursion of the nation-state beyond its borders transfers both control and power to U.S. businesses involved in the trade. Mexican producers and *mangueros* rely on capital infusions from U.S. distributors, creating often unbalanced control of both product and marketing. Crucially, this illustrates how border sanctions, thought to be strictly tied to the territorial imperatives of the nation-state, now extend beyond the border and form part of an all-encompassing global order.

CHAPTER 2

Chiles, Credit, and Chance: An Ethnography of *La Maroma*, Global Finance, and Middlemen Entrepreneurs

Mexican *chileros* balance scarce resources, especially capital, through *la maroma*, a term they use to describe how limited amounts of capital are balanced and extended to maximize buying activity throughout Mexico. The term *maroma* is of Arabic origin and refers to the act of, or engagement in, a perilous undertaking. To "andar en la maroma" is to balance oneself on a tightrope (Velazquez De La Cadena, Gray, and Iribas 1972, 429). For *chileros*, *la maroma* is a dangerous and insecure activity. A successful outcome depends on the skill and cunning of the entrepreneur. Unsuccessful outcomes bring sure and sudden failure—like a tightrope walker falling to death from a high wire. The risk is great, but without it there would be no performance.

Chileros use *la maroma* to manipulate the intensive capital requirements of their business. They balance payments to producers, buyers, and truckers to allow them to participate in the market and export trade. *La maroma* exemplifies the rich excitement and the precarious danger of the *chilero's* life, where thrill and risk are part and parcel of the business. "It gets in your blood," they say, "and it becomes a part of you."

La maroma demonstrates how transnational practices produce discrete and specific local inflections. Transnational patterns that make their presence felt *everywhere* are not necessarily experienced in exactly the same way *anywhere*. The centralized power and economic rationality that guide the expansion of global capitalism often impel local entrepreneurs to act irrationally, boldly, and even romantically as they try to overcome nearly insurmountable obstacles. Yet, in some cases, shared cultural understandings and precise local knowledge can give undercapitalized entrepreneurs on the periphery a temporary advantage over their better capitalized competitors from the metropolis. What seems like inefficient local custom from far away may look more like rational deployment of scarce resources from close up.

This chapter focuses on the activities of Mexican middlemen entrepreneurs in the chile trade conducting business in a transnational market. It starts at one packing shed in Tijuana, Baja California (Norte), and then moves on to examine the actual purchasing of chile in production areas throughout Mexico for export to Los Angeles. There has been a good deal of scholarly work outlining the importance and place of entrepreneurial middlemen and their strategies in market situations (e.g., Babb 1985; Bonacich 1973; Bonacich and Modell 1980; Adams 1970; Acheson 1985; Plattner 1983, 1984, 1985b). Similarly, there has long been a sophisticated genre of work on the proliferation of small-scale commodity production across the global (capitalist) economy (e.g., Cook and Binford 1991; Cook 1984) and the penetration of capitalism into local situations (Nash 1993; Ong 1987, 1992). The case presented here is meant to be a contribution to this established ethnology of global marketing and capitalist activities. But it is one that explores the every-day strategies used in conducting business. Rather than merely adding to the broader confirmation that middlemen entrepreneurs are tied to a global capitalism, I intend to illustrate here how such middlemen engage in the transactions of global capitalism as particular responses to a specific transnational market. Of particular importance here are the actual uses and configurations of global finance and economic services and the cultural logic that forms the basis of business activity.

Elsewhere, I have described the cultural system of *chileros* (chile entrepreneurs and specialists), illustrating the importance of the Mexican institutions of fictive and actual kin, business teams (*equipos*), loyalty, and patron–client relationships (Alvarez 1990, 1994; see also chapter 3 in this volume). These institutions form the basis of risk management and they structure business relations.

The fundamental catalyst of the system, however, is finance. This includes the management of capital and the use of the global services that allow commodity exchange and distribution. Finance encompasses seller–buyer relations in the entire trajectory of Mexican chile, including production, distribution, and consumption, and is inseparable from cultural perceptions and strategies inherent in this trade. Banking, credit, purchasing, and payments for products and services are tied to the specific requirements of *la maroma*. This fact sets the context for the manipulation of global banking services, negotiation with regional and local personnel, and the conduct of distribution activities.

Chile specialists use the term *maroma* to refer to the floating of capital. *Chileros* delay actual payment through a variety of mechanisms that allow the exporter to stretch buying power with extremely limited funds. One might buy two freight loads of product with the capital for only one, for instance, in the hope that sale of the first will help pay for the second. In participating in such activity, the *chilero* must develop a new sense of space and time—being acutely aware of banking procedures, variations in procedures by different banks, capital access, and other information that is carefully manipulated and coordinated.

La maroma, in fact, conditions the entire system in which the *chilero* functions. Viewed as a principle and an ideology to which the *chilero* adheres in daily and long-term business activity, *la maroma* in and of itself becomes a reward and goal of the *chilero*. Successful management and manipulation of capital demonstrates a high degree of skill and knowledge that is recognized and rewarded with prestige and power in "el mundo del chilero" (the world of the chile entrepreneur). As a specific activity of balancing capital in business negotiations, *la maroma* produces only part of the equilibrium for which *chileros* strive. *La maroma* is, in fact, the balancing act of the *chilero* on the tightrope of global economics.

Chileros engage in the export of chile from Mexico into the United States as part of a global trend in the production of fresh fruits and vegetables. The world export of produce has grown 3 percent per year since 1979, reaching 41.5 million metric tons and valued at $18,600,000 in 1988 (Buckley 1990, 17). Fresh vegetables into the United States are Mexico's third-largest export and revenue-producing activity (Banamex 1993).

Although much of this export activity is controlled by large capital-intensive firms (transnational U.S. and large Mexican firms), the production and marketing of certain crops has not been absorbed by North American transnationals. Chile is one such commodity that is controlled by Mexicans. The growing consumption and demand for chile in the United States, however, have encouraged large investments in Mexican middlemen and buyers (see Alvarez 1994). In fact, North American distributors rely on the expert knowledge of Mexican *chileros* and the system in which they function for the produce they seek (Alvarez 1994; see also chapter 3).

The popularity of chile and the high demand for the product are primarily the result of the increase in the numbers of people from chile-eating countries who have made the United States their home (Alvarez 1990; Hamel and Schreiner 1988). The increasing demand for ethnic produce in U.S. urban markets is related to the continued growth of ethnic communities settling in urban centers. Census figures for Los Angeles demonstrate this growth. To be of Euro-American descent in Los Angeles means to be part of a shrinking minority. Today, ethnic peoples make up more than 50 percent of the city's population. Immigrants from Mexico, U.S.-born Mexicans, and immigrants from elsewhere in Latin America and from Asia have changed the face of the metropolis. Los Angeles's Latino population increased 57.3 percent in between 1970 and 1980 compared to an increase of only 5.5 percent in the city's total population (Light and Bonacich 1988, 4). Over the past decade this increase has continued. Los Angeles's Latino population increased 49 percent in the decade of the 1990s. Of the 9,500,000 individuals estimated by the U.S. Census in 2000 to live in Los Angeles County, some 4,200,000 were of Hispanic origin (U.S. Bureau of the Census 2005). Of this total, 3,000,000 or 71 percent were reported to be of Mexican descent. The Asian and Pacific Islander population represented 12 percent of this total, 1,165,000 individuals. For much of this population, chile is a basic part of the daily diet. In addition to the growth of ethnic populations, culinary diversity in U.S. eating habits has also encouraged and popularized the chile (see Alvarez 1994). For example, chile salsa now outsells catsup in the United States.

Most chile enters the Los Angeles market at the Port of San Ysidro, one hundred miles south of L.A. on the U.S.–Mexico border. This port is the largest single-entry land border crossing in the world. In 1988, more than 13 million vehicles and 41 million people crossed the combined ports of San Ysidro and Otay Mesa. In an average year, twenty-five thousand produce trucks enter California, a figure that has grown since the adoption of NAFTA. More than 440 million pounds of produce entered the United States through this port in 1988. Of this total, chile ranked fourth in volume after tomatoes, strawberries, and squash (products that are consumed by the general public) (Olson 1988, 1). Chile is thus a high-volume commodity and is highly significant in the market activity of Los Angeles. Chile is the only such commodity that is demonstrably tied to the new ethnic populations in the United States (Hamel and Schreiner 1988).

As a volume commodity, chile has fostered entrepreneurial activities throughout Mexico that are dependent on global services and finance and are now an integral part of the global marketplace. The activity of *chileros* as middlemen entrepreneurs in a global market warrants explanation because it varies from the usual perceptions about the world system creating uniform dominance and dependency, as Frank (1969) and Wallerstein (1974) argue. Although the chile market does sometimes fall into the dependent–dominant relationship between core and periphery, in the case of chile this is a fluctuating situation in which the nature of the product and its distribution play a significant role. Indeed, there are times when the Mexican chile middlemen dominate the market.

Insofar as Mexicans control the distribution of chile, transnational corporations in the United States have become dependent on the *chilero* system for obtaining the product. As suggested by Canclini (1995), the core–periphery relationship is inverted here because of the cultural knowledge held by Mexicans in what would be considered the periphery and because of the ways it enables them to control part of the process of chile production and export. The highly intensive capital wholesalers of the Los Angeles market do not always dominate the small, capital-poor entrepreneurs across the border in Tijuana, because although *chileros* are dependent on the Los Angeles market for continued sales and long-range security, they continue to control the distribution of *chile* into the United States. This control resides in the cultural capital that builds relationships and trust among producers for the buying of the product, and the teams (*equipos*) of buyers who work the republic for the *chilero* entrepreneur (Alvarez 1994; see also chapter 3).

The nature of the Mexican market for chile is also important in the *chileros'* control of distribution and it often offsets the disadvantages that *chileros* face in the Los Angeles market. Most Mexican chile goes to the United States, but increasingly, large shipments of fresh green and some varieties of dried chile (the Mexican *chile japonés* or Japanese chile) go to China and Japan. These markets remain underdeveloped, but are becoming more important. Yet Mexico still consumes the major portion of this product. Even more important, Mexico continues to be the production and consumption capital of commercial varieties of chile (Long-Solis 1986). Indeed, some Mexican *chileros* prefer to sell *nacional* (in Mexico) because of constant Mexican demand and the vulnerability and variability of the U.S. chile market (Horcasitas 1988).

Unlike the *chilero* who sells solely in Mexico, the exporter relinquishes a good deal of product and market control by venturing into the U.S. market. American firms are known for their ruthlessness and attempts at control (Horcasitas 1988). Hence, the Los Angeles market, like other global market places for chile, is often secondary in a hierarchy of dominance and control. The Mexican demand for chile provides an outlet for Tijuana entrepreneurs, thus weakening the control of American distributors in Los Angeles. The Tijuana *chileros* have focused on export because of the strength of the dollar, but they also sell to local markets. Tijuana is a large metropolis in which, as in the rest of Mexico, chile is essential to the daily diet and where outlets exist for chile of the finest (export) quality as well as of poor quality (*resaga*—the leftover). Tijuana has seven large wholesale markets and more than thirty smaller fruit and vegetable markets. This is important for the exporter because it offers both a secondary market in times of low demand in Los Angeles and a primary outlet when demand and prices skyrocket in Mexico.

Indeed, there are periods of product scarcity during which sales in Mexico are more profitable than export sales. Without the local market, the large companies in Los Angeles would clearly dominate and control the distribution of chile.

It would not be accurate, however, to say that the *chilero* exporters of Tijuana are not in some ways dependent on the wholesale companies of Los Angeles. The prices in Los Angeles are a major gauge for the activity of *chileros* in obtaining product. Furthermore, the financial strength of Los Angeles in making payments and extending credit to *chileros* induces exporters to rely on the L.A. market. Indeed, this financial dependency has been noted as a principal weakness of Mexican fruit exporters by the Confederación Nacional de Organismos de Productos de Hortalizas y Frutas (the major Mexican union of produce growers and exporters) (Horcasitas 1988). The dependency is not one-sided, however. *Chileros* know that Los Angeles is dependent on Tijuana for the distribution of chile. The stiff competition among *chileros* themselves for shares of the L.A. market has been a major barrier to better control on their part. Some *chileros* recognize this weakness, as evidenced by the building of a Central de Abastos (a central market) in Tijuana in 1995, built in part to set standards and fair prices and to protect the exporters from the growing dominance of American firms.

The interdependency of the L.A. and Tijuana markets provides *chileros* with a certain amount of freedom to secure products and manipulate resources. The real dependency of the *chilero* stems from the global services that condition local, regional, and hemispheric activity in the distribution of specific commodities. This dependency ties Mexican entrepreneurs to the global economy and financial institutions. Chiles are grown year-round in Mexico (Alvarez 1994); and because production follows a seasonal cycle, Mexican *chileros* must try to control vast geographical areas to procure their product. The crop comes from as far away as two thousand miles from the U.S.–Mexico border at certain times of the year, and from as close as a hundred miles at other times (see Figure 1). *Chileros* shipping to Los Angeles from Tijuana must secure product from the states of Baja California Norte and Sur, Sonora,

Chihuahua, Sinaloa, Zacatecas, Guanajuato, and others. They must establish marketing relationships with farmers throughout the country, and expend capital and resources in these areas throughout the yearly growing and marketing cycle.

The Empacadora Fronteriza (a pseudonym) packs and exports chile at a location situated on the U.S.–Mexican border in Tijuana. Full tractor-trailer loads, from 20,000 to 35,000 pounds each, arrive at the Empacadora from throughout Mexico. The product is unloaded, washed, boxed, weighed, and sent to a variety of wholesale distributors in the Los Angeles Wholesale Terminal. During 1987, the Empacadora shipped a previously unheard of amount for a Tijuana company (as many as ten loads) to the L.A. market—close to 300,000 pounds of chile per week. The market value of each shipment varied from twenty-five to thirty-five thousand dollars depending on the type of chile and its availability in the marketplace. (At low times of the year, two to three loads—approximately 25,000 to 75,000 pounds per week—were exported.) In addition, chile was sold locally in Tijuana to other exporters and for local consumption.

The Empacadora Fronteriza represents the efforts of a single entrepreneur, whom I will call Juan Verduras. Juan controlled and coordinated a vast network of production areas and managed the financial structure that made it possible to maintain high-volume sales in the Los Angeles market. This included expenditures for representatives of the Empacadora who traveled throughout Mexico establishing contacts and making purchases, bank payments to producers, telecommunication (telephone and money orders), and transport costs.

The firm began as a joint venture between Juan (a Mexican *chilero*) and an American wholesale produce distributor (which I will call Border Distributors). Juan worked with Border Distributors sending truckloads of fruit and vegetables across the border and shipping produce into Mexico with a small fleet of tractor trailers that he had acquired over a period of several years. In addition, Juan worked with a Mexican partner who was the principal buyer for the Empacadora. In 1982, when the Mexican peso suffered drastic devaluation, like many Mexican *fruteros*, Juan was left with huge debts that he was unable to pay. The peso lost value against the dollar, and debts incurred in the United States to American wholesalers were the first to go unpaid. A number of Tijuana exporters went bankrupt because of their loss of capital resulting in indebtedness.

Juan had established a good working relationship with Border Distributors, however, and he felt obliged to pay the debt he had incurred buying produce. He offered his equipment (his tractor trailers) as payment. The owner of Border Distributors, impressed by Juan's offer, worked out a collaborative agreement; rather than taking Juan's primary means of business and livelihood, he joined with him in a Mexican export venture. The Empacadora would operate independently but would provide export produce and other services for Border Distributors. Credit and other help would be forthcoming from Border Distributors to ensure the successful operation of the packinghouse and export business.

Juan secured a plot of land in central Tijuana with nearby access to the international border's commercial entry point into the United States. The land was located in a burgeoning *colonia* of settlers new to

Figure 1. Mexico and the chile-sending region.

Tijuana. Once established, the Empacadora attracted more newcomers and spurred the growth of the *colonia* because of its informal status as a "fuente de trabajo" (source of work). Once in full operation, the Empacadora employed as many as seventy-five workers.

The company purchased equipment from a tomato-packing plant that went out of business just across the border in Otay. A tomato washer and sorter along with a transportable warehouse approximately 100 by 250 feet was disassembled and taken to Tijuana. Friends of Juan's assembled the shed and sorter at virtually no cost. Juan often joked that the Empacadora was the only packinghouse in the country that cost only a few cases of tequila to build. The Empacadora started full operation once a loading dock of cement and basic facilities for the *empaque* (packing shed) workers were built.

Juan ran the entire operation with the help of crews who had little or no education. He took it upon himself to identify and train individuals suited to a variety of tasks, including record keeping, bill collecting, quality control, and other jobs. He nurtured good employees and often said that the future of any business rested in the people it employed. He controlled all phases of the business, supervising the plant operation, sales, and the *traileros* (drivers of the semitrailer rigs used to haul produce). An entrepreneur in the truest sense, Juan had working and practical knowledge of mechanics (diesel and gasoline), tractor-trailer driving (he had driven most of the Mexican roadways), refrigeration, packing, trailers and tractors, agriculture, and the marketing of Mexican produce.

The *empaque* workforce consisted of a variety of employees organized around tasks that included unloading product, washing and sorting, packing, weighing, stacking and loading, box repair, and maintenance in the yard and the shed. In addition to these manual tasks, Juan employed several bookkeepers who kept track of the operation, including inventory control, accounts payable, and banking. One woman, who became Juan's administrative assistant, coordinated much of this work, managing a small team of two or three women who kept track of inventory, employee workdays, and other minor accounting tasks. The majority of the workers lived in the immediate *colonia*.

Juan often operated the *empaque* contrary to American business standards. For example, American firms often discourage the hiring of multiple kin, but Juan frequently employed two or three members of the same household. This provided a relatively secure income for some families.

Juan also attempted to keep as many people as possible employed. He realized that his contributions to the families and to the *colonia's* development could secure the loyalty of his workers and was part of a larger business strategy that incorporated employees into *equipos* (teams) (see Alvarez 1994 and chapter 3). His strategy for the *empaque* required a large labor force for processing chile in times of high demand. The business logic was to build and maintain a high volume of quality export product. In the long run, he could offer lower prices and provide high quality while ensuring a steady supply for the large wholesalers in Los Angeles. It also meant that the firm would be able to secure markets and provide continuous outlets for producers in times of high and low demand. This meant maintaining large numbers of employees even during periods of low-volume sales. Juan engaged the workers in a number of jobs around the *empaque* while he labored to increase the volume of chile buying throughout the country.

Buyers were the most important employees, because Juan depended on them for product. All work in the *empaque* relied on incoming produce supplied by buyers working in production areas throughout Mexico. During times of high demand, Juan had as many as three buyers in the chile-producing areas of the country (Alvarez 1991, 1994).

Buyers lived in Tijuana, and, like the employees from the *colonia*, often came from agricultural and rural working-class backgrounds. These individuals earned relatively modest salaries and identified with the working classes of the *colonias*. Juan himself had little material wealth and lived a modest life in Tijuana. The rewards of playing *la maroma* and its attendant lifestyle, however, provided numerous social rewards in addition to the possibility of "hitting it big" and reaping large monetary rewards.

The long-distance trailer drivers also played an important role in the business. Most had worked for Juan for years, and advanced upward through the ranks from loaders to drivers, although occasionally drivers were hired from outside the circle of loyal employees (see Alvarez 1991, 1994; see also chapter 3). The *traileros* drove primarily into the interior of Mexico, yet one or two were needed to cross merchandise from Tijuana into the United States for the Los Angeles market. These latter drivers had the most prestigious jobs and received the best pay because of the extra skills and documents needed to cross the international border. Both passports and a working knowledge of the U.S. markets were necessary (see chapter 3).

The *empaque* was a Mexican border operation. Its ranks were filled by a labor pool of working-class individuals. Few in the *empaque* had much schooling—those who had begun secondary school were a rarity. Most were drawn from the immediate *colonia*. Employees spent much of their time on the grounds. Frequent fiestas and barbecues, and even occasional dances for employees and other *colonia* residents, were held there. The *empaque* was viewed as a community benefit, a "fuente de trabajo," and became a major landmark and identifier of the *colonia*. In one episode, the *colonia* residents protested the attempted rezoning of the plant grounds, which would have required relocation. More than two hundred residents marched on the government offices in downtown Tijuana protesting the possible relocation of the *empaque* because of its value to the community. The business had provided numerous jobs and had spurred the development of two household restaurants (one of which was owned by a prominent community leader). The community viewed it as a resource, not only for jobs but for other benefits as well.

Buyers representing the Empacadora travel into chile-producing regions and work with farmers to develop both economic and social bonds in order to secure a reliable source of supply. The buyers become key figures who handle cash and resources in ways that benefit both themselves and the farmer. As one *chilero* in Tijuana explained, "el comprador es la bujilla del negocio" (the buyer is the spark plug of the business). In essence, the buyers make the business "run" by maintaining relationships with farmers, accessing chile harvests, and building an economic base that ideally gives them a greater level of control.

As Juan does in Tijuana, the buyers in the field utilize *la maroma*.

Usually, this entails making a few cents' profit over the actual price. If, for instance, a load of jalapeño costs the buyer twenty-five cents a pound in the field, his earnings are included in the buying. It is assumed, however, that most buyers will add to the buying price, inflating it to "earn" more than previously agreed upon. This is a recognized cost that exporters like Juan are willing to absorb. This practice keeps buyers working contentedly to assure product delivery. Yet this becomes a matter for negotiation between buyer and *empacadora* when market prices become exceedingly competitive or profitable. These few cents are also negotiable between the buyer and the farmer. Thus the buyer, representing the *empacadora*, builds in a flexibility that allows maximum leeway in buying. The bottom line, however, is the procurement of chile that is competitive in the export L.A. market.

Although buyers have a base pay that is used for personal expenses, they also have access to large sums for chile purchases (transport, labor, advances to farmers). These sums are paid at the discretion of the buyer, who is in control in the local buying region. In 1985–87, Juan sent almost 433 million pesos (roughly 150,000 dollars) to one buyer. Buyers are known to reinvest some of this capital, when possible, for personal gain. Like Juan at the packing shed, the buyer plays *la maroma*, carefully balancing the high costs of failure with the possibility of success.

The relationship between the buyer and the *empacadora* is an economic and negotiable one. Juan relies on the buyer for product; the buyer shows his loyalty through continued efforts in procuring chile, using the capital and resources at his disposal both to secure product supply for the *empacadora* and for his personal gain.

The buyers for the Empacadora began their careers under the tutelage of Juan at the *empaque*. They learned the necessary skills and proved their loyalty during years of service. The buyers in the time period discussed here began working for Juan as adolescents. They were familiar with the firm's operations and with its need for timely deliveries and quality product. They moved up from working as warehouse workers to becoming long-distance drivers of semitrailers and acquired experience in the buying areas, often negotiating for the *empaque*. Juan recognized their talents and promoted their apprenticeships as buyers, first training them on buying trips, and later sending them on short but important business trips into the interior. Buyers formed part of the central team of the *empaque* and enjoyed secure positions in the business.

Most producers are small landholders who specialize in growing chile. Buyers work closely with these farmers to gain their trust and to establish long-term relations to ensure a regular supply of the product. Well-known producers become the target of intense competition between buyers from different export businesses. Often exporters and buyers from the markets of Mexico City, Guadalajara, and Monterrey compete for the loyalty and product of small individual farmers. (I focus on this buyer activity in more detail elsewhere; see Alvarez 1994.) Most producers are campesinos who work with little capital. Although a few large landholders worked hundreds of hectares (especially in Guanajuato, a traditional chile-producing region), most farmers worked relatively small parcels of land. Many of these farms are family-run and rely on family labor for most tasks.

The fact that producers rely on kin and kinship ties is a crucial factor in understanding why American firms have been unable to control the chile market. Americans do not attempt to invest in or build long-term relationships with producers, often switching loyalties as markets and supplies change. The small producer relies on the buyer/exporter for market access and thus, like the buyer, hopes to form long-standing relationships in order to secure outlets for his product.

Operating capital for the *empacadora*, as with most exporters, comes from both initial and continuing credit sources. Juan Verduras, for example, became aligned with a strong Los Angeles firm that advanced capital for chile purchases. He was known for his astuteness and his ability to procure product, as well as for his technical knowledge of cross-border transport. In addition to credit he received from the Los Angeles wholesaler, he borrowed large sums of money from *prestimistas* (individual loan sharks), friends at *casas de cambio* (money-exchange houses), other *fruteros* (fruit entrepreneurs), and relatives. Bank loans were inaccessible to him because of low or nonqualifying collateral. He secured loans nonetheless, totaling thousands of dollars at interest rates as high as 80 to 90 percent a year, and has made interest payments of as high as fifteen thousand dollars a month.

Meeting interest payments alone requires a constant source of capital through high-volume sales and vigilant manipulation of personnel, capital, product, equipment, and other resources.

Short-term credit from producers is another important component of the operation. Once buyers in the southern region establish themselves and gain credibility (through timely payments), producers often provide product on short-term credit and consignment. Producers are often paid advances to cover the immediate expenses of harvesting, with the understanding that full payment will be sent when the chile is sold.

Thus, *chileros* use personal and business loans through informal sectors, and seek credit from producers, to maintain their buying and distribution operations. This is not capital accumulation but the utilization of capital resources—human capital, commodities, and cash value.

In addition to credit and loans obtained through the informal sector, distributors also utilize the formal banking system. Deposits in local branches of the national banks, both Banco Cremi and Banamex, serve to pay local and regional costs, but other banks are utilized in production areas as well. Bank services extend buying power and include services such as money orders and checking accounts. Money orders are sent throughout the buying regions for purchases as well as for the basic expenses of buyers. Because cash accounts are often insufficient (for amounts of capital requested by buyers) daily deposits are made to cover money orders. On a daily basis, *chileros* send out couriers to collect debts and to borrow cash from trusted *fruteros* with whom they are in good standing. Once enough capital is collected, bank deposits make money orders possible, and *pagos de orden* (payment orders) are sent to buyers through regional bank branches.

Checking accounts are utilized in a variety of ways. Checks allow *chileros* to meet obligations to clients without an immediate expenditure of capital. They also make it possible to extend limited funds and delay payment, and the use of different banks allows maximum flexibility for such transactions. For example, the management of capital for one load of chile arriving at the Empacadora Fronteriza from Guanajuato required payment to the driver for transport and payment to the producer for the chile being transported. On active days, more than one load, and as many as three or four loads, would arrive at the Empacadora, and each load required payment. Checks to cover transport costs were given to the drivers of the tractor rigs or ten-wheelers (*torton*) to be delivered to their respective companies. The travel time to the production area was calculated in making the payment, giving Juan three to four days before the check would be cashed. Depending on the bank on which funds were drawn, this might take another three days for processing. Therefore, more than a week's time was "bought" before the actual capital was required for payment.

Although Juan gave some cash to the drivers for expenses and as good faith for payment, these amounts were usually much less than actual billing for transport and product. In essence, a sum of forty thousand dollars could be used initially to cover up to three times that amount. *La maroma* allowed Juan to meet the Empacadora's immediate obligations, but also to continue distribution and purchasing.

In addition to banks in Tijuana that were used for money orders and checking, accounts in other banks were utilized in the production areas. There, buyers held checking accounts and paid both advances to producers and later payments, once product was sold, from nonlocal banks. This allowed immediate payment in the eyes of producers, but, like the transactions for transport, these were calculated by *chileros* in such a way as to allow the use of limited capital for further purchases and expenditures on the part of both the buyer and the Empacadora. The actual processing time of specific banks was calculated into payments to producers. Thus, a payment in Guanajuato on checks for a branch of the Banco de Atlántico in another location might take three days to process, in addition to the time it took the producer to deposit the check in a local bank, thereby buying time for the *chilero* in Tijuana and extending the available capital. Consequently, both the location of banks and banking procedures became crucial to *la maroma*.

Like other *fruteros* in the Tijuana market, *chileros* are dependent on the use of telecommunication services for electronic bank orders, communication with production regions, and information about the activities of competitors. Although the telephone has been in use for decades, the volume of activity, interdependency, and the crucial timing of calls for market activity are paramount in this transnational market.

In 1987–88, Juan placed a total of 2,848 calls from the Empacadora Fronteriza to both the United States and Mexico. Approximately half of these calls were to Mexico (1,426), while the other half were placed to the United States (1,422). A total of 6,700,000 pesos (about three thousand dollars) were expended on these calls. These did not include calls placed to the Empacadora from long-distance locations or local calls. The calls to the United States were to Los Angeles and San Diego, indicative of the daily selling and distributing. An average of eight long-distance calls per day were made throughout the year. The Empacadora kept close contact with Sinaloa, Zacatecas, Guanajuato, Guadalajara, and the other sending regions in Mexico (see Table 1).

In addition to the calls made from the Empacadora, buyers in the south remain in continual communication, through phone calls as well as travel, with production regions in an effort to maintain relationships and create new sources for product. (In most cases buyers use a pickup truck provided by the *chilero* for travel.) In 1987, in addition to a principal buyer stationed in Guanajuato, Pascual—a buyer representing the Empacadora—traveled from Tijuana throughout the states of Sinaloa, Nayarit, Jalisco, Michoacán, and Colima contacting producers, establishing contacts, buying product, and reporting on the activity of competitors throughout the region. This included almost daily telecommunication with potential sources of product, with the Empacadora in Tijuana, and with the Guadalajara market—a key indicator of chile prices in Mexico. During a five-month period, the traveling buyer made more than 120 long-distance calls to various states. Of these, 32 percent were to the Empacadora in Tijuana and 22 percent were to the Guadalajara market. The remaining calls were to twenty-one cities throughout the production region including Tepic, Culiacán, Los Mochis, Manzanillo, El Rosario,

Table 1. Number of calls to specific Mexican locations, with cost in pesos

Area code	Location	Number of calls	Pesos
14	Chihuahua	82	191,486
15	Gomes Farias	4	6,574
16	Nuevo Casas Grandes	19	23,784
17	Torreón	2	1,056
18	Durango	8	6,468
32	Tepic	95	94,787
33	Tecomán	132	628,353
34	Tamazula	5	18,167
35	Zamora	3	11,853
36	Guadalajara	256	550,643
37	Teocaltic	12	21,464
45	Zacapu	5	22,449
46	San Luis de La Paz	84	375,434
48	San Luis Potosí	3	8,005
49	Fresnillo	67	193,039
55	Mexico City	4	8,518
56	Mexico City	2	1,414
57	Mexico City	3	11,258
62	Guaymas	12	21,329
63	Nogales	11	22,815
64	Huatabampo	38	77,300
65	Mexicali	116	66,677
66	Ensenada	74	23,948
67	Villa Unión	155	596,778
68	Los Nochis	179	296,728
74	Acapulco	42	212,212
83	Monterrey	3	20,568
84	Parras	1	3,081
86	El Madrid	1	5,924
91	Ejido Coatill	1	2,213
110	Rincón de Tamayo	7	14,353

Mazatlán, Esquinapa, and San Luis Potosí. (These calls totaled 382,612 pesos, about two hundred dollars.) The Empacadora also made bank deposits totaling 1,923,526 pesos (about ten thousand dollars) for other immediate costs to the buyer, primarily telecommunication services.

The activities of this buyer illustrate the complex nature of regional communication, and the necessity of face-to-face interaction of northern *chileros* with small producers in the production regions. Not only were calls to and contacts with producers from Tijuana necessary, but the presence of a representative in the region is crucial to maintain continued access to the product.

Travel costs for Pascual included hotels, gasoline, and repairs for the pickup. His costs (in addition to his base pay) totaled 3,679,111 pesos over this period (approximately fifteen hundred dollars). This illustrates the persistent involvement of the northern exporters with producers and production regions throughout Mexico. The Empacadora had two roving buyers in addition to a principal buyer in the southern region during the most active production periods of the year. This presence would be impossible without the use of global telecommunication systems and modern transport.

In addition to the costs of reconnaissance and communications, the immediate expense of actual chile buying remains paramount. Between 1985 and 1987, approximately U.S.$150,000 were sent by money order to southern regions for the purchase of chile (see Table 2). One buyer controlled this capital. This represented direct money orders and did not include cash sent with trucks of the Empacadora to the buyer, payments by check in Tijuana, or payments from individual checking accounts held in local southern banks. The destinations of the money orders follow the growing season throughout the production region and illustrate the movement of the buyer (see Table 3). Two states in particular, Sinaloa and Guanajuato, illustrate the intense focus of the Empacadora and this particular buyer in establishing ongoing buying relationships with producers: in 1985, 4,400,000 pesos (approximately U.S.$210,000) were sent to Sinaloa; in 1986, 22,600,000 pesos (approximately twelve thousand dollars); and in 1987, 231,633,509 pesos (approximately U.S.$110,000).

The Empacadora's greatest strength with farmers, however, was in the state of Guanajuato, where *chile pasilla* is grown in San Luis de La Paz. The firm was the first of the Tijuana packing exporters to ship this region's chile to Los Angeles. In 1985, 20,900,000 pesos (approximately U.S.$10,500) were sent in money orders here. The following year, 1986, 120,805,000 pesos were sent (approximately sixty thousand dollars). In 1987, this figure doubled. In addition to money orders, cash was delivered by drivers of Empacadora trucks; for example, in one season, 6,520,000 pesos (approximately U.S.$3,500) were sent to one buyer alone (Zacatecas). Similar cash deliveries were made to all buying states. The Empacadora used six Mexican banks during this period, at times simultaneously and interchangeably.

Chileros like Juan from the Empacadora Fronteriza manipulate large amounts of capital skillfully. "Es capital muy fuerte" (It is very strong capital), noted one exporter in appreciation of how *la maroma* gets the most out of every peso and dollar. Profit for most *chileros* is viewed in terms of a revolving source of capital that allows ample reinvestment so they can continue to walk the high wire. If a *chilero* is skilled enough and perseveres despite the "fuertes caídas y subidas" (sharp upswings and downturns of the business), he might be able to capture high sales and high profits. The trick and thrill of the game lies in continuing the performance.

Table 2. Total money sent to Mexican states, in pesos, October 1985–April 1987

State	Money orders	Pesos
Baja California	4	1,290,222.43
Distrito Federal	2	3,889,814.45
Guanajuato	41	141,681,801.22
Jalisco	1	1,002,693.30
Sinaloa	26	258,504,948.60
Zacatecas	23	26,606,496.98
Total	97	432,975,986.98

Of crucial importance is how the Los Angeles market actually responds and what the possibilities are of capitalizing when prices are high. A careful look at the market prices of chile in the Los Angeles market indicates that the market is relatively steady and predictable. During 1983–88, prices remained relatively stable in Los Angeles, with high prices peaking at predictable times of the year (for instance, during Lent, when Mexican Catholic tradition forbids the consumption of meat and demand for chile goes up). Only on rare occasions did the prices jump to extremes (United States Department of Agriculture 1983, 1984, 1985, 1986, 1987, 1988). On these occasions, chile was scarce and available from producers at inflated prices, negating any real profit for exporters. High, unpredictable prices in Los Angeles were the result of unforeseen events during which chile was not available (for example, weather and border closings). The point is that the likelihood of windfall profits for *chileros* in Los Angeles is very small. The *chileros'* hope is that through the continued manipulation and balancing of resources, a chance to hit that window of opportunity for windfall profits might arise. Only rarely have *chileros* profited in strong markets, and when they do, their profits are usually short-term and not sustained. The majority of *chileros* have yet to rise above the goal of *la maroma* of balancing resources and playing

Table 3. Total money sent to Mexican states, in pesos, 1985–87

State	February–December 1985	January–December 1986	January–April 1987
Baja California	1,290,222.43	0.00	0.00
Distrito Federal	0.00	3,889,814.45	0.00
Guanajuato	20,877,462.22	120,804,339.00	0.00
Jalisco	1,002,693.30	0.00	0.00
Sinaloa	4,342,718.60	22,528,731.00	231,633,509.00
Zacatecas	13,842,818.98	12,763,678.00	0.00
Total	41,355,915.53	159,986,562.45	231,633,509.00
Monthly average	3,759,628.68	13,332,213.54	57,908,377.25

the game. Like the tightrope walker, many have fallen. The turnover of exporters because of bankruptcy is very high.

Producers of chile in Mexico are tied to a *specific* transnational market in the global economy. The social trajectory of chile as a commodity in the markets of Mexico and the United States revolves around global services, especially finance. These precarious and complex ties depend on the manipulation of capital through a number of financial and human resources. In addition, *chileros* use time and space (see Gupta and Ferguson 1992) in the equation of successful marketing. Delay and geography become integral factors in this transnational activity.

High finance and modern global services are intimately tied to a logic that is used in the manipulation of these activities. *La maroma* is an interpretive strategy encompassing large capital, banking, and credit. The high-wire act of the chile exporter is not only a game of chance involving credit and high finance, but also a defining characteristic of the perspective and goals of *chileros*. Finance, banking services, and the logic of *la maroma* tie the *chilero* of Tijuana to a transnational market and the global economy.

The actions of *chileros* such as Juan and his buyers are important in understanding not only how business is conducted, but also how entrepreneurs interpret and manipulate global finance at the local level. Specific local and regional knowledge about financial institutions and financing is crucial, and the cultural interpretations of such knowledge illustrate unique uses of time, space, and human resources.

The implications for NAFTA are multiple. Growing American and Mexican trade necessitates a better understanding of local business systems and cultural logics illustrated by *la maroma*. Of crucial importance here is the way in which capitalism engages and is engaged by activity at the local level. As capitalist enterprises, and capitalism in general, penetrate manufacturing and production, conflicting ideologies and behaviors result. The local-level interactions of commerce in NAFTA, and the actual business activity by entrepreneurs and producers, managers, and labor, are of crucial importance.

CHAPTER 3

The Long Haul in Mexican Trucking: Traversing the Borderlands of the North and the South

Trucking is one of the most significant ways people enter into capitalist economies as entrepreneurs. Yet trucking has been little studied in its own right, much less in relation to the trajectory of capitalist development and its curious contemporary irony, that the more capitalism brings peoples together, the more ethnically differentiated they seem to become (Appadurai 1990; Hannerz 1990). Truckers in Mexico's north and south, entering the "borderlands" of their respective regions, forge new forms of ethnic solidarity in the trucking business, thereby gaining advantage for their burgeoning enterprise even in the face of dominant alien commercial practices.

Throughout Mexico, truckers partake of the image and reputation of the macho folk hero of the road. Songs and stories celebrate the Mexican trucker as a kind of folk hero. Cabin and bumper slogans (Edmonson 1959; Jaquith 1974) emblazon his values (in Mexico, trucking is exclusively a male role, except in the popular Mexican movie *Lola, la trailera*, which features a female trailer truck driver as its protagonist). The trucker seems to command the highway, disdaining the danger for which Mexican roadways are notorious, and relishing adventure, spontaneity, women, and tequila, all the while sacrificing for the good of the family he maintains and supports.

There are nonetheless noteworthy differences in both the style and the organization with which Mexican truckers and merchants transport goods to and from markets. Northern Mexican truckers self-consciously draw on networks of personal relations and patronage in the transport of fresh fruits and vegetables to markets in the United States. Indigenous Mayas from Mexico's southern highlands, by contrast, emphasize corporate organization and legitimation of their transport of fruits, vegetables, and flowers within their region and from markets in central Mexico. Although we begin by exploring the commonalities and differences between these two groups, our purpose is to underscore the emergent and culturally productive processes through which each set of entrepreneurs deploys business activity as an ethnic enterprise in the borderlands. By calling attention to cultural style as a fundamental aspect of the way in which Mexican truckers successfully do business in alien domains, we suggest that the kinds of interchanges likely to be newly stimulated or augmented by NAFTA (the North American Free Trade Agreement or *Tratado de Libre Comercio*) will not be simply economically motivated but will depend as well on the culturally engaged and distinctive ways in which peoples do business.

Recent developments in social and cultural theory (Rosaldo 1989) and increasing attention to problematic traditional identities (Clifford and Marcus 1984, 23) have given new salience to borderlands, to the interstices between conventionally defined peoples and societies, and to the increasingly transcultural and transnational processes that shape our world. But in problematizing peoples' identities, borderlands also afford them the space within which to constructively reassert who they are, how they differ from others, and what place they claim for themselves.

By "borderlands," our colleagues refer not just to the physical spaces at the conjunction of national frontiers but to the sites that potentially can be found anyplace where distinct cultures come together in interaction without thereby losing their differences. In our analysis of northern Mexican trucking, the Los Angeles wholesale markets are as much a "borderland" because of the way they juxtapose and confront Anglo and Mexican ways of doing business, as the actual U.S.–Mexico frontier that Mexican truckers cross through in Tijuana. Highland Maya truckers, exemplified by the truckers we have studied in Zinacantán, traverse and renegotiate the border that has historically disadvantaged the access of indigenous ethnic peoples to markets and enterprise dominated by ladinos, their region's non-Indian Mexicans.

Borderlands confront peoples with sometimes poignant ambiguities of identity that evoke polyvalent senses and possibilities of being. Gloria Anzaldúa (1987, vii) speaks of "keeping intact one's shifting and multiple identity and integrity" as "like trying to swim in a new element," an "alien" element. Guillermo Gómez-Peña writes of the multiple repertories of his identity in the Tijuana–San Diego borderland: "I am Mexican but I am also Chicano and Latin American. On the border they call me *chilango* or *mexiquillo*; in the capital, *pocho* or *norteño*; and in Spain *sudaca* . . ." (as translated in Rouse 1991, 8). Such polyvalence allows for playful experimentation with guises and roles, as in the case of a Maya truck driver we know who posed for his portrait as a driver in *norteño/tejano* (northern Mexican/Texan) attire, as a *sherif* (sheriff), and as a *contrabandista* (drug runner). People can hide behind the ambiguities of identity, as did another Maya trucker who, after fleeing an accident for which he was at fault as driver—stylishly dressed for driving in *norteño* attire—used his ethnic garb for disguise as an indigenous truck owner in negotiating with authorities for release of his impounded truck. But the ambiguities of identity in borderlands can also be strategically played upon to forge, reformulate, and even mobilize ethnic identity to advantage, as Mixtecs have done in migration for work at and beyond the U.S.–Mexican border (Nagengast and Kearney 1990).

In both cases of entrepreneurial Mexican trucking that we shall describe, ethnically disadvantaged truckers from less-developed domains nonetheless monopolize some kinds of trade in the wealthier, dominant societies and markets to their north. They manage to do so, in part, by elaborating the style and organization of their businesses as ethnic enterprise. The northern truckers draw upon characteristically Mexican interpersonal reciprocities and patronage to meet the challenges of transnational business. Indigenous Mayas of Zinacantán, in organizing their trucking, tap their repertory of corporative ideology for organizing community life. Anthropologists have often considered the structuring of trade along ethnic lines as a response to risk and as a strategy for gain (Plattner 1989, 181–82). We want to invert the implicit causality of an economistic interpretation of ethnic trading as an adaptation to risk by emphasizing instead that culturally different entrepreneurial styles can in themselves give rise to *different* ways of managing "risk." Thus we will underscore the emergent and culturally productive processes through which each set of entrepreneurs deploys and extends ethnicity in their borderlands.

The image of borderlands also invites us to reconsider the conventional image of "community" as bounded space within which social relationships, even if differentiated, converge around integrated life ways or draw shared understandings from practices that take shape in a given habitus (Bourdieu 1977). Transnational capital development increasingly draws people into diaspora even as production moves offshore. Networks and archipelagos become ever more apparent in the circulation of people, along with goods, money, and information, across places in ways that forge new kinds of translocational spaces. Mexican migration to the United States, for example, began with pioneers who forged "network" or "circuit" communities (Kearney 1988; Massey et al. 1987; Nagengast and Kearney 1990; Rouse 1991) that enabled later migrants to move more safely within far-flung social spaces that span problematic frontiers. Although these spaces may become "familiar," the ability of newcomers to make them so should lead us to question how conservatively rooted peoples' possibilities are in the practices shaped by habitus.

We will point out that Maya truckers reconfigure the space in which their compatriots conduct petty commerce, effectively extending the ethnic community into formerly alien markets and expanding the meanings of ethnicity. Much as the "networks" or "circuits" of northern Mexican migration made it possible for relatives and friends, even women and children, to join in, so Zinacanteco truckers have opened up once-alien markets throughout their region to the petty commerce of ethnic compatriots, women as well as men. Northern truckers, analogously, have reconfigured the Los Angeles wholesale produce markets as ethnically differentiated places that are nonetheless safe for ethnic trade.

Because of their inherent mobility, truckers—like tourists—deserve more of our attention as agents of what Gupta and Ferguson (1992, 10) describe as "the irony of these times . . . , that as actual places and localities become ever more blurred and indeterminate, *ideas* of culturally and ethnically distinct places become perhaps even more salient." In this chapter we are calling attention to some of the political-economic underpinnings of such reterritorializing of identities in the borderlands.

Our discussion of trucking in the north concentrates on the marketing of produce at the Los Angeles Wholesale Terminal from across the California–Mexico border, a wholesale-retail network in which one of us (Alvarez) has direct entrepreneurial experience. We examine the way in which the northern Mexican produce entrepreneurs (*comerciantes*) deploy and elaborate personal networks of kinship, reciprocity, patronage, and trust—the sorts of horizontal and vertical ties that Lomnitz (1982) and Vélez-Ibáñez (1983) claim are characteristic of Mexican urban society—as a distinctive style of doing business that helps them penetrate the alien commercial markets of Los Angeles. In the case of Maya trucking in the south, where both of us have undertaken ethnographic research among the highland Maya, we focus on the trucking and distribution of produce by entrepreneurs of a specific ethnic community, Zinacantán. Zinacantecos distribute produce to and from the central highlands of Chiapas, including long-haul wholesale transport from central Mexico's largest produce markets. Here we see marketing and transport that draw upon more corporatist organization and ideology that enable Zinacantecos to extend their enterprise as ethnic trade in the world of markets formerly dominated by non-Indian Mexicans. In both cases, ethnic entrepreneurs are affording compatriots the opportunity to enter into borderlands in enterprise that expands and extends the significance of ethnicity.

The Development and Scope of Northern Trucking

Each year, thousands upon thousands of trucks enter the United States to haul fresh produce to distant wholesale market terminals at a rate that has increased since the passing of Mexican–U.S. trade agreements in

1994. Unknown to most, this is a complex and intensive commerce for which hubs in both Mexico and the United States often compete (Alvarez 1989, 1990). Trading is highly competitive and requires the produce *comerciante* to know about the varieties of each product, where and when it will come into season, how it can be shipped in time to markets where demand is strong, and how to juggle the labor and huge, risky investments of capital needed to trade competitively.

After characterizing the development and transnational scope of this trucking and underscoring its risks and competition, we will center our attention on how Mexican truckers use cultural resources of patronage, *confianza* (trust), family ties, and *compadrazgo* (godparenthood) to mitigate and manage competition. Then we will follow the expansion of their produce trade into the Los Angeles wholesale markets as ethnic enterprise.

Northern Mexican trucking and trade in produce date from early in the twentieth century, reflecting the long-standing orientation of northern Mexico's commercial agriculture to export. Until the 1950s, northern Mexican produce responded primarily to demand for crops such as oranges, tomatoes, and strawberries that complement and supplement those that are only seasonally available in the United States. Beginning in the 1950s, the Mexican produce trade began to respond to the food preferences of the burgeoning Latino populations in the United States, beginning in urban areas such as San Diego and Los Angeles that were relatively close to the border, and then spreading throughout the United States.

We concentrate our attention on the produce trade that flows through Tijuana from Baja California Norte and Sonora into the markets of Los Angeles. Much of this trade is in tropical fruits and vegetables such as mango, chile pepper, tomatillo, jícama, cilantro, nopal (cactus), tuna (prickly pear), and other goods that cater to the tastes of Latinos living in the United States. Mexican *fruteros* (a self-designation of fruit and vegetable entrepreneurs) began to bring such produce from Tijuana markets into Los Angeles in the 1950s, supplementing produce grown locally in the Los Angeles and San Diego areas. Don Jaime, a respected and aging local *frutero*, boastfully remembers his entrance into the market at this time: "I arrived at the [Los Angeles] market when there were no chiles and named my price." As the market for Mexican produce expanded beyond the San Diego–Los Angeles area, however, the demand soon outstripped local supply. *Fruteros* in Tijuana with access to produce throughout Mexico began shipping into the Los Angeles Wholesale Terminal, a major distribution center of produce throughout the United States.

Although shipping through the border at Tijuana into Los Angeles is similar to that through other commercial crossing points along the international border, there are subtle differences. Nogales is the border place through which the largest volume of Mexican winter vegetables flows into the United States, whereas Tijuana (which is our focus) channels a continuous flow of produce into Los Angeles throughout the year. The lower Rio Grande Valley of Texas, particularly the MacAllen border area, imports large volumes of cantaloupe and other fruits that are processed and packaged by large firms in the area. Los Angeles, however, is the largest wholesale market terminal in the United States catering to the largest Mexican immigrant population, as well as to a growing multiethnic market. Unlike shippers who export to Nogales, primarily a distribution point for large-scale American brokerage firms, the markets of Tijuana specialize in Mexican produce aimed at the ethnic trade in Los Angeles, which in turn serves as an entrepôt for supplying such produce north to San Francisco and east as far as Chicago.

Demand from the United States taps production deep within Mexico and depends on Mexican shippers and growers for supply. Produce flows from throughout Mexico following the seasonal growing cycles. Chile peppers, for example, are grown and shipped north from Sonora, Sinaloa, Jalisco, Michoacán, Guerrero, and Baja California at different times of the year (Alvarez 1989). Mangos follow an analogous pattern of routes and seasons. As a result, the transnational fresh produce trade has become highly differentiated. Vendors specialize in particular kinds of produce, acquiring their commodity from all kinds of growers throughout Mexico and then using truckers to transport the product to buyers who concentrate on supplying particular markets. Truckers work for the vendors, sometimes as employees, but sometimes under contract as independent operators, usually on a full-time basis.

The relationship between entrepreneurs (buyers, vendors, and distributors of product), on the one hand, and truckers and other transport workers, on the other, is often difficult to sort out. The difficulty stems in part from how tasks combine, especially for entrepreneurs who enter into the produce business on a small scale. Some enter the trade as owner and operator of a vehicle—as small as a one-ton pickup—purchasing, transporting, and selling the product without assistance. Most individuals see the tasks of distribution (buying product, hauling, packaging and sale, and shipping to the U.S. market) as an integral part of the larger role of being a *comerciante* in the export produce business. As a business grows, these primary tasks become too burdensome for any one person to handle and the *comerciante* will bring in others to assist and to perform specific tasks. At this stage, he may own one or more large tractor-trailer rigs or small one-ton pickup trucks and will hire drivers and helpers. Or he may contract with truckers on a regular basis. Trucking roles are thus integral to the produce industry and to the community of *comerciantes* to whom truckers are linked.

As the *comerciante* is defined by both product and role, so too are truckers identified by roles within the transport and distribution system. Roles include *chóferes* (drivers), *fleteros* (freight haulers), *troqueros* (truckers), and *transportistas* (shippers). Hence, transport and trucking are embedded in a network of distribution tasks encompassed in the overall marketing performed by *comerciantes*, who in turn have the major responsibility for all tasks associated with distribution and marketing. To this end, individuals who have learned to drive and have become *chóferes* or *fleteros* often aspire to the *comerciante* role. Indeed, the actual participation of individuals as "truckers"—as *fleteros* or *transportistas*—is seen as falling within the entrepreneurial domain of the *comerciante*.

The knitting together of roles can be illustrated by the arrangements for shipping produce through markets in Tijuana into the United States. There are more than seven markets through which *fruteros* conduct such business. The Mercado Miguel Hidalgo is the largest and boasts the most successful entrepreneurs. These *comerciantes* purchase high volume in truckloads to meet the increasing demand across the border. Most have set up independent warehouses to receive, clean, and pack product to U.S. standards before it crosses the international border. These *comerciantes* have teams of workers *(equipos)* to meet the complex demands of export. Indeed, each *frutero* and his *equipo* form a tight partnership, spending the majority of their time working the product together. The *chóferes* (like other workers) spend their time around the *puesto* (market stall) or *empaque* (packing shed) helping in all activities. In addition to actually driving, *chóferes* (like other employees) also help clean and sort, load and unload product, work on their vehicles, and run important errands. Theirs are full-time efforts that entail twelve- to fourteen-hour days, six days a week. They even spend time off with working partners. The individuals who form parts of *equipos* become full-time participants who, like the *frutero*, speak of their life as "la vida del comerciante" (the life of the produce trader).

The relationships among trucking and produce entrepreneurs and workers in their teams are difficult to generalize about in terms of class.[1] Individuals active in the produce trade range from those who hold or wield substantial amounts of capital as *comerciantes* to those who are involved initially solely as employees.[2] But the produce trade involves many people of intermediate or ambiguous position who also undertake roles in which they may be working their way up as part owners of trucks and workers in the employ of a *comerciante* who aspire to becoming independent *comerciantes* themselves someday. Although shippers for some northern Mexican agribusiness units are unionized, as in the case of the Baja California cotton transporters affiliated with the Confederación Regional Obrera Mexicana (CROM, Mexico's largest labor federation), in ways that might sharpen class identity, the shippers we speak of are not.

The *comerciantes* of the north are Mexican nationals from throughout the republic. Although many come from families that originally traded fruits and vegetables in their native states, most now range far afield throughout the north and across the border. Rather than specializing in products of any given region, they focus their efforts on a product line. Success in distribution and marketing depends on knowing where and when to obtain the product, how to handle, pack, and transport it while controlling for quality, and how to deliver it quickly and safely to extend its "shelf life" after it has reached markets. Because specific goods have different characteristics, distributors (truckers and vendors) usually dedicate themselves to certain goods. Most consider themselves *fruteros*, which refers to the handling of fruits in general. However, most *fruteros* specialize in specific types of fruits or vegetables, such as tomatoes (*tomateros*), chile (*chileros*), or onions (*cebolleros*), drawing on expert knowledge of variations in the type, seasonality, regional availability, and pricing of their chosen crop (Alvarez 1990). We use the term *frutero* in reference to all produce entrepreneurs. The economic behavior of Mexican *fruteros* plays a vital role in the incorporation of immigrants into the larger labor market, an incorporation that is now part of a transnational process. They purchase produce from throughout Mexico following seasonal changes and production of crops. The *comerciantes* compete for product from independent growers with *pequeña propiedad* (small private landholdings) as well as from members of *ejidos* (communally held land).[3] The larger-volume businesses also buy from established growers who control large tracts of land either through ownership, rental, or lease. Large grower-brokers will often establish contracts with small farmers who are unable to participate in the export market. In essence, the *comerciante* takes advantage of all possible sources of product.

Much of the northern commerce spans the U.S.–Mexican border in complex and competitive marketing arrangements. Entrepreneurs in northern commerce usually align themselves with U.S. wholesalers, who in turn supply vast American and Canadian markets. The enormous demand of these markets affords opportunities for substantial profits to those who can purchase goods with cheap Mexican currency and sell them for U.S. dollars. Northern Mexican commerce, as a result, is highly competitive, tempting even small vendors with pickups or small trucks to compete with shippers who deliver full trailer loads of specific goods to U.S. wholesalers.

Although the industry affords opportunities for large profits, it also entails considerable risk; the market is highly competitive, the price and availability of produce vary seasonally, regionally, and often unpredictably, and produce can readily perish. The risks are similar to those noted for the distribution of produce and highly perishable commodities in other markets (see Plattner 1989). Shippers must secure goods whose supply varies by region, season, and the vagaries of weather. They must sell or dispose of the produce before it spoils. Mexican *comerciantes* who would compete in U.S. markets face additional risks. The Perishable Agricultural Commodities Act mitigates losses from spoilage for U.S. merchants but not Mexican competitors. Mexicans trading in the United States also must cope with crossing the international border and complying with U.S. customs and regulations for product and equipment.

Patronage, Trust, and the Management of Competitive Risk
Whatever their specialty, these northern shippers face steep competition and high risk, their success or failure often pivoting on the unexpected or the unknown. In addition, the capital they need for business usually draws on all their savings and liquidity, and on borrowed funds as well. Although the potential for profit in the trade is great, so is the entrepreneur's risk. Shippers attempt to manage the risk of failure by investing in and developing relationships with others in the trade who can help in times of stress or, in the event of drastic losses, even help them start anew.

We find that relationships embedded in the asymmetrically reciprocal loyalties of patronage are common in northern trucking, relationships in which more secure entrepreneurs offer support to others as *patrón* (boss). *Comerciantes* often develop this type of patronage of "their" truckers in the north. Although some independent *troqueros* own and drive their own vehicles, most throughout Mexico and in the north affiliate themselves as *chóferes* (drivers) to private businesses, often to a specific *patrón*.

The affiliations usually arise over time as novices work their way up in an entrepreneur's shipping business. Many of today's drivers started out working as youthful apprentices, learning the trade from the bottom up. A shipper might take on a young man in adolescence as a favor to a relative or friend, starting the novice as a packer or loader, and gradually rewarding loyalty and hard work with advancement and greater responsibility in the business. Eventually, the proprietor might entrust the employee with driving the business's vehicles, and he might even assist the driver in becoming independent.

The case of "Mochis," a young driver who worked at La Empacadora Tijuamex (where one of us, Alvarez, was affiliated), illustrates this advancement. Mochis (nicknamed after his home of Los Mochis, Sinaloa) began working at the packing shed, helping to load and unload trucks and sort chile peppers, the primary product of this business. Because of his hard work and loyalty, he was first allowed to drive the company vehicles around the adjacent yard, then to take daily trips to the city dump, and was finally "given" a truck to drive for long-distance hauling from Sinaloa and Guanajuato when chiles were purchased from those areas. In time Mochis crossed the border into the United States and became part of the export team.

In such a relationship, lasting bonds of trust and friendship form in which *transportista* and *comerciante* rely on each other in ways that go beyond any contractual bond, helping each other as opportunity and need arise. Relations and constraints of trust have been described in markets between buyers and sellers in cultural settings other than those described here. Similar market relationships have been explained as ameliorating high risk in perishable goods (Plattner 1989; Acheson 1985; Wilson 1980). One could well argue that the high risks entailed in produce markets favor affiliations that go beyond purely economic transactions and in which entrepreneurs invest in personal relationships such as those marked by trust. We would argue, however, that risk cannot in itself give rise to the specific kinds of relationships that mitigate it. Rather, in the case of north Mexican shippers, *comerciantes* draw on and elaborate a cultural repertory of interpersonal relationships, including that of *confianza* (trust), which Vélez-Ibáñez (1983) has discussed as having distinctive Mexican significance.

In their businesses, *comerciantes* extend *confianza* beyond dyadic contracts with specific sellers or buyers in local marketing situations to embrace far-flung relationships in the greater community of the produce trade. Mexican *comerciantes* use and identify *confianza* as a means to secure relationships of loyalty with workers, other *comerciantes*, and even the North American buyers with whom they do business. Indeed, the term *confianza* is overtly used and identified specifically in relationships. As one Mexican *comerciante* put it to us, "Sin la confianza no hay negocio" (Without trust, there can be no business).

The paternalistic and politically charged Mexican relation of the *patrón* to his clients complements *confianza* as a tool in the cultural repertory of relationships that *comerciantes* bring into their businesses. *Confianza* loyalties sometimes consolidate entire teams of individuals who work together under the auspices of a *patrón* who in turn sees them as "mi gente" (my people). Other *comerciantes* will recognize these "teams" as "gente de fulano de tal," that is, John Doe's people. Within such teams, boss and workers expect absolute loyalty from one another. Although individuals may change jobs and bosses, the loyalties themselves may continue, as, for example, when José Verdad, a Tijuana *chilero*, went broke and his previous team continued helping him even though they were now employed by a competing employer. The loyalty to this particular *chilero* is especially evident in the assistance he received from one of his former *chóferes*. Juan Verduras, an established *cebollero* in Los Angeles, had learned the onion trade from José. When Juan was a young boy, José took Juan in, taught him to drive, and provided him with his first opportunity to drive tractor-trailer rigs, finally making it possible for Juan to buy his own rigs and to work in the Los Angeles market. When Juan learned of José's ill fortune, he gave José one of his two tractor trailers and told him, "Trabájalo, y págame cuando puedas" (Go to work [with the rig], and pay me when you can). He expected no payment for the use of the equipment and was explicit about helping José as he had been helped in the past. Such loyalty is not uncommon in the *equipos* of *patrones*.

We see Mexican patronage and trust as used by *comerciantes* as responding to two kinds of difficulties in the highly competitive northern trucking and produce industries. First, shippers face seasonal and cyclical variations in the volume and profitability of their businesses. Second, truckers are vulnerable to unpredictable losses and even failures. When business slackens in winter, or when products are not available, entrepreneurs and their workers are said to have to *aguantar*, or endure adversity, by sticking it out together until better times. When disastrous losses cripple a trader, he will expect others to return the favors he granted them in better times, for example, by asking employees and affiliates to work without pay. The social capital of patronage thus complements and sometimes even replaces tenuous commercial capital.

Patron–client ties in the manner described here emphasize the mutual help and loyalty that are needed to secure market and reduce risk, but these ties are asymmetrical in that *patrones* command obligatory relationships of workers that become embedded in expressed forms of loyalty. Workers are at the beck and call of their *patrón*, dependent for work and wages and the possibility of any advancement and favors. The use of such power by *patrones* varies with individual personalities, but among the range of *comerciantes* who must depend on such social relations, exploitation of workers is rare. As businesses grow and accumulate capital, relations between *comerciante* and worker become less personalized, and exploitation of employees becomes evident. Workers may shift allegiances or become competitors once free of obligations. However, most workers align themselves with particular *patrones* for long periods.

The patron–client relationships we have been describing are not unlike those that economic anthropologists have identified as equilibrating market relationships generally in situations that involve high risk (Plattner 1985a). One has only to remember Sidney Mintz's (1961) description of Jamaican *pratik* partnerships or Clifford Geertz's (1978) Moroccan bazaar trading to evoke a host of examples in which traders limit risks and secure business via such patron–client ties and relations. Yet once again the relationships we see in northern Mexican shipping strike us more as enactments of Mexican personal and political relationships found both in and outside of enterprise, spanning kinship and politics in a wide variety of institutions and contexts, such as those to which Lomnitz (1982) has called attention.

Relying on patronage, northern shippers also enact other values and practices that inhere in many Mexican institutions and sociocultural relationships. Enterprises often draw on the expected solidarities of *familia* (family) that bind together networks of kin extending across the international border (Alvarez 1987). *Confianza* may extend into friendships that *compadrazgo* (godparenthood) cements into enduring relations of extended fictive kinship. Family firms have been built up on such loyalties. What is notable is not simply that northern business should build on such values, but rather that such values have endured in the highly complex and modern entrepreneurial marketing of the north.

In calling attention to the culturally Mexican repertory that *comerciantes* deploy in their businesses, we seek to avoid either essentializing or idealizing. Mexicans are not categorically constrained to use patronage, *confianza*, *compadrazgo*, and *familia*, but they constructively choose to do so in the northern produce trade. They may do so to secure loyalty and credit, and relieve business setbacks from within their networks, but they also use such relationships to delimit outsiders from insiders in competition and to control subordinates.

Thus relationships important in forming and maintaining business transactions cannot categorically be taken for granted. *Confianza* can, on occasion, be short-lived or contoured by market fluctuations and demand. A conversation between two merchants about a series of loads of Mexican produce illustrates the manipulation of *confianza*. In order to continue packing and shipping, the Mexican *comerciante* (a shipper of mangos) was requesting prepayment for loads that were not yet shipped across the border. The American buyer (a Mexican-American) indicated that there was to be no prepayment: market prices had dropped and the risk of not being able to sell future loads was growing. The Mexican asked, "Qué pasó con la confianza?" (What happened to our trust?); the answer was, "Aquí no hay confianza, solamente pura lana" (Here there is no trust, only hard cash). Disappointments between *comerciantes* can break down *confianza* or reorient patronage. What is significant is that the north Mexican *comerciantes* nonetheless deploy their cultural repertory and distinctive styles of doing business in ways that mitigate and manage the risk and competition inherent in their venturesome transnational businesses.

Traversing the Northern Borderlands in Mexican Enterprise

When Mexican truckers cross the northern border into the United States, they confront regulations that differ from and are more stringent than those in Mexico. They also encounter the American popular image of the trucker, who (like the cowboy of yore) should epitomize independence and self-reliance by disdaining dependence on social ties (Agar 1986, 11; Rothe 1991, x). If anything, Mexican truckers draw all the more on their Mexican repertory of personal networks, patronage, and *confianza* as cultural resources in this doubly alienating encounter.

Both U.S. and Mexican law complicate the long haul north. Mexico restricts some exports and requires exporters to repatriate capital. North American regulations, such as the Tandem Truck Safety Act of 1984, impose special requirements and constraints on Mexican truckers who ship into the United States in addition to those that regulate north American trucking generally (Hughes and Peach 1985). To cross the border, Mexican truckers need passports, truck insurance, special licenses, and Interstate Commerce Commission certificates or permits to enter the United States. They also must undergo border inspections designed to enforce hundreds of laws for dozens of different agencies. U.S. agricultural inspectors check imported produce for pesticide content, correct packaging, labeling, origins, and destinations. For certain products, only specific types of containers are allowable in the United States, and truckers often have difficulty obtaining them in Mexico, where wooden and cardboard packaging is not always readily available. Only a minority of Mexican truckers can surmount the complexities and logistical costs of exporting produce to the United States. Those who do must rely on the services of customs brokers on both sides of the border and the knowledge and assistance of others.

In addition to the logistical hurdles of traversing the border, the Mexican exporter assumes extreme financial risk if he has no guarantee that his product will be accepted in an alien market. Only shippers who can secure contacts with buyers north of the border dare to venture northward. Even when a buyer and shipper come to terms over the purchase of produce or requisite quality from specific *fruteros* for timely delivery, their deal can sour if the trucker's vehicle breaks down or if customs or USDA inspectors reject the shipment.

Even more than in northern Mexican trucking generally, those who venture into the United States resort to characteristically Mexican entrepreneurial networks. They link themselves up to compatriots in U.S. markets who understand and use the cultural relationships on which Mexican businesses rely. Unlike the *chóferes* in Mexico, who sometimes work independently as free agents, the truckers who enter the United States work for specific bosses. Even those Mexican truckers who become independent haulers and work for freight payment are regular haulers for specific businesses and entrepreneurs, and are considered part of a *patrón*'s team (*equipo*).

To the aspiring *troquero*, entering the Mexican entrepreneurial system as it has developed in the United States affords access to enhanced opportunity, a better quality of living, and freer range and independence. The Mexican trucker who is able to cross into the United States also gains prestige for entering the unknown world of the United States' highways and markets. Upwardly mobile Mexican truckers seek out relationships with compatriots who already export Mexican produce, knowing that these individuals have established networks of working relationships in the United States. They view such compatriots as potential heads of businesses and future patrons, insofar as many do start up new businesses of their own. Thus the long haul northward into alien markets actually accentuates and elaborates the stylistic distinctiveness of Mexican entrepreneurial organization in the northern borderlands.

In many aspects of organization and entrepreneurial style, Mexican truckers shipping into the United States differ markedly from North American truckers who either work for a salary or on rates based on distance (Agar 1986; Rothe 1991). North American independents who own or lease their own rigs hire out on a contract basis. North American truckers generally limit their responsibilities to hauling. They leave loading and unloading to warehousemen or distributors who accept produce to deliver to local markets. North American truckers, especially those who drive semis long-distance, generally belong to unions that protect their rights and limit their work to the specific task of driving. North American truckers bring kinship into their organization in the husband–wife teams (Rothe 1991, 99–108) that enact nuclear family models of independent enterprise. By contrast, the Mexican trucker organizes in terms of real and fictive patriarchal kinship. The Mexican trucker's networks of loyalty involve him in many more shipping activities. Most Mexican drivers assist in loading and unloading cargo. As a representative and extension of the *comerciante* for whom he works, the Mexican trucker will even collect his patron's debts, or undertake to buy or sell the patron's produce for him if a deal falls through. *Chóferes* thus take on multiple roles that integrate the personal networks by which Mexicans enter into alien markets. Although Mexican truckers sometimes work independently south of the border, those who would meet the logistical challenges of transborder shipping must invoke networking and patronal support.

When the *troquero* enters into U.S. commerce and trucking, he does so through distinctively Mexican channels. Mexican *fruteros* dominate the dense network of Mexican produce vending in the Los Angeles markets. Indeed, a hierarchy of Mexican markets exists in Los Angeles, ranging from those that sell to the small-scale vendors who deliver in neighborhoods throughout the city to those that distribute to large North American chain stores. The market hierarchy and dominance of Mexicans has the character of an ethnic enclave parallel to those described by Portes and Bach (1985; see Alvarez 1990). The *troquero* rarely meets North American drivers, and when they do meet it is usually in packing sheds or at the delivery docks of wholesalers. *Troqueros* frequent the numerous Mexican restaurants and neighborhoods. English is rarely spoken, as even most North American firms employ buyers and vendors who speak Spanish and hire other workers from a predominantly Mexican or Mexican-American labor pool to deal with the Mexican *comerciantes* and *troqueros*.

The ethnic enclave that these Mexican traders have grasped in the Los Angeles markets is reminiscent of the "middleman" position that ethnic minorities have occupied in many contexts, notably in trade and commerce, but also in mediating between producer and consumer, elite and masses, employer and employee. Edna Bonacich (1973; Bonacich and Modell 1980) links such intermediate roles to minorities who hold on to their identities even while attaining intermediate status that evokes the hostility of the dominant society and perpetuates a reluctance to assimilate. We would argue that such ethnicity in the borderlands of Los Angeles gives Mexican traders a certain comparative advantage.

Thus, in terms of ideals, the very characteristics that make the Mexican trucker appear marginal to his North American counterpart are in fact what make him viable, if distinct, in the borderland produce trade. To North American truckers who idealize independence and self-reliance and eschew obligations beyond those of driving, the networks embraced by Mexican truckers seem compromising. From the North American standpoint, Mexican truckers appear to work on a shoestring, being constantly in need of quick payment. They see Mexicans as using trucks that seem antiquated and deficient. By contrast, from the Mexican perspective, those who cross the border own the best Mexican trucks (as evidenced by their actually meeting stringent U.S. safety codes), they have tapped into networks that afford them the greatest liquidity in capital, and they are most experienced in deploying the reciprocal relationships of give-and-take with workers and bosses—and even with North Americans—on which venture into alien markets depends.

In actuality, the Mexican system of cultural resources is becoming as significant for North American companies that deal in Mexican produce as it is for Mexican entrepreneurs. This is especially so because of the growing integration of the U.S. and Mexican economies and the burgeoning Mexican and Latino immigrant populations in areas such as the Greater Los Angeles metropolitan region. One can anticipate that the NAFTA has intensified these trends. The high demand for Mexican produce has drawn North American firms into Mexican networks for procuring produce. Large North American businesses tap into the Mexican system of reciprocity and mutual help by hiring Mexican-Americans, Mexican immigrants, or other Latinos who speak Spanish and are culturally aware of the system. Thus buyers and proprietors of North American produce firms enter into alliances with Mexican entrepreneurs, even to the extent that some Latino buyers have taken up relationships of *compadrazgo* with Mexican shippers. These relationships are not in evidence among other American firms or with other non-Mexican ethnic groups. Indeed, Mexican *comerciantes* promote such relationships with American firms through buyers in efforts to solidify commercial relationships in the long run. Such North American firms may in turn become middleman distributors that help Mexican entrepreneurs gain access to more distant markets in the U.S. interior, which is beyond the legal reach of Mexican trucking. Some North American firms even adapt their business practices to Mexican needs, for example, in paying for merchandise on a biweekly or weekly basis instead of every twenty-one days in the manner of U.S. chain stores. Mexicans, in turn, have come to depend on these firms for reliable purchase orders and ability to supply financial capital readily.

The importance of the use of cultural resources is especially evident in the Mexican entrepreneurs who have established themselves in the Los Angeles market. Most of the Mexican *comerciantes* there began by hauling produce into the Los Angeles market while relying on personal networks and contacts with other Mexicans already in the market. In 1986, the city of Los Angeles opened its new and modern Los Angeles Wholesale Terminal market facilities for produce, covering some forty acres. As large, established North American businesses moved from older produce markets into the new terminal, Mexicans and other non-Anglo entrepreneurs moved into the vacated markets. The entire complex, however, is part of the Los Angeles market. The old Seventh Street Market (one of the two larger markets vacated) became primarily a Mexican market, as former Mexican haulers leased stalls there, alongside Mexican entrepreneurs for whom they once shipped. American firms that moved to the new terminal maintain market stalls here (often under different business names) to compete for the Mexican trade.

Although Mexican *comerciantes* have established themselves in the Seventh Street Market, they continue to face the market dangers of high risk and low capital. Bankruptcy and turnover are high. Meanwhile, some of the more ambitious Mexican entrepreneurs have set their sights on penetrating even the new terminal because it is there that the largest volume of trade, the greatest security of payments, and longest-term business transactions lie.

The Los Angeles Seventh Street Market exemplifies how "successful" Mexican entrepreneurs in turn attract other Mexican truckers and entrepreneurs into their expanding networks (see Alvarez 1990). Of the thirty-six businesses in the Seventh Street Market in 1988, twenty-six specialized in Mexican commodities. These businesses rely on their own teams for locating, buying, and packing produce in Mexico and shipping it north. Once across the border, Mexican truckers follow Interstate 5 between Tijuana and Los Angeles, the primary route by which produce flows into the Los Angeles terminal market. The traffic of these *fruteros* is impressive on the eve of strong market days, as truckers loaded with chile peppers, cilantro (coriander), tomatoes, onions, and other Mexican specialty produce rush to meet delivery deadlines. Trucks of all sizes dot the highway, each easily identifiable by the Mexican slogans on bumpers and doors, the colorful, brightly painted cabs, and the packers' and shippers' personal box labels. Pickups, larger ten-tonners, one- and two-ton bobtails, and the ever-impressive brightly lighted rigs of the *traileros* stand out as cultural artifacts of the system to which they belong. Although the high turnover in these businesses reflects the exceptional risks of transnational trade, their continuing entrepreneurial pattern is organized in the culturally Mexican style that relies on personal networks, patronage, and *confianza* to manage risk. Like the Zinacanteco of the south (to whom we now turn), these northern *troqueros* have elaborated ethnic strategies and distinctive cultural resources to claim and establish their place at the borderland of an alien commercial world.

The Development of Southern Trucking as Regional Enterprise

The trucking undertaken by highland Mayas in southern Mexico is different in many respects from trucking in the north. Trucking has a shorter history in the south and responds to more limited and less stable demand than in the north. Overall, southern trucking is less specialized than in the north and more embedded in a regional economy. Shippers in the south use long-distance hauling to supplement produce grown locally and distributed primarily within the region outside their communities of origin. Many Mayas use shipping to supplement peasant farming, or they combine trucking and vending. Most carry passengers as well as produce.

The social and economic organization of transport in the south is also different from that in the north, reflecting the indigenous emphasis and ideology of communal solidarity and collective action as well as the corporatist strategies that the PRI (Partido Revolucionario Institucional) has used to regulate economic and political activity in the region. Thus the specialization of goods does not take place at the level of individual entrepreneur but at the level of ethnic "township" (*municipio*), as in the case of Zinacantán, with its ethnic specialization in flower vending throughout the region. Further, vendors generally combine with others from their ethnic community to trade in regional markets. Groups of six to eight vendors who share a market stall in one of the region's cities or towns rotate responsibility for transporting and selling their pooled produce.

Long-haul trucking developed later in Mexico's south than in the north and with an orientation that is much stronger to the regional than to the national economy. Mexico completed paving of the Pan American Highway through the Isthmus of Tehuantepec to the Guatemalan border only in the 1960s. Southern produce merchants did not tap central Mexican wholesale markets until the 1970s. Whereas shippers of the north orient their businesses to passing goods through the *frontera* into the United States, southern shippers primarily go to central Mexico to bring goods to the southern border region in which their businesses are embedded.

A mango deputy (USDA inspector) holding mango with heat sensor. Altamirano, Guerrero, 2002.

Mango deputy checking sensors as mangos in Weld boxes are lowered into hot-water tanks. Altamirano, Guerrero, 2002.

Mango packing line. Altamirano, Guerrero, 2002.

Semitrailers and trucks in northern Mexico. Esquinapa, Sinaloa, 2002.

Zinacanteco in traditional huipil with his truck. San Cristóbal de las Casas, Chiapas, 1991.

Chumula trucker at home. Chumula, Chiapas, 1991.

The author with his father, Robert Alvarez Sr., at the School of American Research, 1995.

Wedding photograph of Tiburcio (Tom) Castellanos and Refugio (Ruth) Sotelo. San Diego, California, 1928.

Two of three primary corridors of the forty-acre Los Angeles Wholesale Terminal.

The Seventh Street Los Angeles "Mexican" Market.

One major contrast with the north is that southern transport is much more deeply tied to the southern regional economy, to the extent that regional producers, even peasants, participate significantly in transport. One sees semis and trailers on the roadways in the south involved in commercial transport that is probably similar to that of the north in its organization and social relations and how it serves new and expanding commerce. But southern trucking is predominately that of smaller vehicles serving the agrarian production of farmers and peasants. This contrast with the north is owing in part to the historic preponderance of peasant agriculture in the south and the north's historic orientation to commercial agriculture and ranching (as well as mining) for export. A more recent development in the south has drawn agrarian producers, including nonethnic peasants as well as ethnic Zinacantecos, into trucking and produce trade as entrepreneurs who have taken over much of the small-scale wholesale and retail produce trade in regional markets.

Our case study of southern trucking and ethnicity focuses on the produce traders of Zinacantán. Zinacantán is one of some twenty Tzotzil- or Tzeltal-speaking *municipios* (townships) in the central highlands of Chiapas. The peoples of the highland townships contrast with non-Indian Mexicans of the region, who dominate urban business and commercial farming and ranching. The highland townships that are indigenous, peasant communities are also ethnically distinct from one another. Indigenous trucking began in the 1960s, promoted in Zinacantán and other Indian townships by Mexico's Instituto Nacional Indigenista (INI).[4] The transportation business in Zinacantán is probably the most developed of these highland townships. Zinacanteco trucking has burgeoned more than elsewhere in part because of the community's strategic location along the Pan American Highway between two of the region's principal commercial cities, San Cristóbal de Las Casas and Tuxtla Gutiérrez. Zinacantecos' early involvement in long-distance produce transport via mule and horses and the community's greater entrepreneurial wealth also contributed to the development of transport businesses using trucking. Not, thus, a typical case, Zinacantán's trucking nonetheless exemplifies how substantially Indians of the region have become involved in motorized produce transport both within the region and as far afield as Mexico City.

As links to national markets grew, three kinds of development drew peasants and indigenous groups of the region, such as the Zinacantecos, into produce trade and trucking. First, agencies that fomented economic growth and change among indigenous communities, such as the INI and the Programa de Desarrollo Económico y Social de Chiapas (PRODESCH), built roads and helped peasants from indigenous communities to buy trucks. Second, by favoring the construction of feeder roads after 1978, as opposed to earlier building of trunk routes, the national state opened up once-remote agrarian regions. But the major impetus came from the third development: tapping new sources of energy, in three major hydroelectric dams on the Grijalva River and the Tabasco oil fields, in the process drawing peasants and Indians out of the countryside into construction jobs and commerce.

We ourselves witnessed the development of energy infrastructure and the way it drew the Zinacantecos of highland Chiapas into commerce and trucking in the 1970s and early 1980s (Collier 1990, 1992). The Zinacantecos were not total newcomers to produce transport, having in some instances made livelihoods by hauling cargo by mule train within the region. But from the time of agrarian reform in the 1930s, most Zinacantecos had centered their livelihoods in farming milpa— until the 1970s, when jobs and commerce in the areas of oil drilling and dam building drew them out of agriculture. Many then took up unskilled wage work in construction at unprecedented salaries; others undertook wholesale and retail vending of produce to the developing sector; and a minority invested in vehicles to transport people and produce for profit. Although the post-1982 economic crisis curtailed construction and commerce, sending many workers back into peasant agriculture, many Zinacantecos nonetheless have continued in the wholesale and retail trade and the transport of produce as at least an adjunct to farming, if not as a full-time pursuit.

That an indigenous community of some twenty-one thousand peasants can deploy nearly a hundred trucks and an equal number of *combi* or VW minibuses in regional transport is unprecedented in the *frontera sur.* Vehicles are to be found in every Zinacanteco hamlet, parked next to milpas, at places of ritual, around town centers, and along virtually every roadway in the township. Zinacanteco-run trucks loaded with cabbage, potatoes, other vegetables, fruits, flowers, and people ply the roadways between metropolitan markets of the region in San Cristóbal de Las Casas, Tuxtla Gutiérrez, and Comitán. And they make regular trips to Mexico City's central wholesale markets to purchase flowers to sell in the south.

Truck owners epitomize wealth and power, as in the north, and they also set trends in popular culture in the south that are new to the region. Trucks themselves have taken pride of place next to ownership of land and homes. The truck cabin is the place where the privileged ride and the powerful carry on intrigue. Truckers set fashionable new tastes in clothes by what they choose to wear when on the road. The purchases that truckers bring home introduce Zinacantecos to new commodities and consumption.

The Corporatist Management of Zinacanteco Trucking: Mitigating Risk or Sharing Responsibility?

As compared to northern shippers and truckers, Zinacantecos organize their businesses in shipping much less exclusively toward the making of profit per se. The tempo of northern trucking is much more intense. Northern trucking and transport occupations are full-time. Northern truckers tend to maximize the utility of their vehicles for immediate and long-term profit by hauling as frequently as they possibly can and with the fullest possible loads. Zinacanteco truckers, by contrast, work on limited schedules that appear not to maximize the utility of their vehicles in the same way. Most Zinacanteco truck owners belong to trucking unions and work only on specified days and limited schedules that rotate trucking opportunities among members and restrict any given trucker's profit. Many drivers complain of the costs and unprofitability of working their market route according to schedule because they often have to run at a loss. Why is it, then, that Maya truckers continue in the business when it is seemingly unprofitable? Why do they not better maximize the utility of their vehicles in transport, as do truckers of the north? Why are there so few full-time truckers in Zinacantán, and none who make their living exclusively as long-distance *fleteros* (cargo haulers)?

One factor that accounts for this different entrepreneurial style of Zinacanteco trucking is that the economy of the south may well not support full-time trucking in the post-1982 era of economic contraction. After the national-debt crisis of 1982 reduced gainful employment in construction and diminished commercial activities that Zinacantecos had pursued in the preceding boom, many Zinacantecos reoriented themselves toward agriculture in the highlands, making new use of chemical inputs—fertilizer and weed sprays—to intensify maize cultivation. Today, most Zinacantecos who engage in commerce and trucking also farm. Furthermore, there are seasonal variations in the rhythm of the region's economy and in the mix of profitable activities it will sustain. For example, the market for flowers, which truckers market through the region, peaks at Todos Santos (All Souls' Day) in early November and in the spring during the period from Lent through Holy Week and into early May. It slackens after the June rains inaugurate a new growing season, a time when farmers of the region have to devote cash to the purchase of agricultural equipment and supplies rather than market produce.

Most Zinacanteco truckers are farmers as well and conceive of themselves as farmers, even though they may devote a majority of their time to trucking and commerce. One of the presidents of the two Zinacanteco trucking unions states that he is "100 percent a milpa farmer" even though the majority of his time is taken up in non-milpa farming activity. Trucking and the vending of produce, it seems, supplement farming, filling up people's time during those seasons in which farmwork slackens. Thus the primary purpose of highland Mayan entrepreneurs is not to maximize the profit derived from trucking and flower vending, but rather to have these activities profitably supplement their farming of milpa. Although they range far afield in commercial transport, most Zinacanteco truckers are still firmly inserted in the agrarian production of their homeland.[5] This is in sharp contrast to northern shippers, none of whom are direct producers, although a few may work in partnership with producers.

It is also apparent that the Mexican state's political relationship to Indians and peasants influences the organization of Zinacanteco trucking through the trucking unions, in a way that has no counterpart in the north. The Zinacanteco trucking unions are but one of the many kinds of peasant organizations through which the PRI sustained a measure of control of ethnic communities of the south. The communities have been clients of the state since the time of agrarian reform earlier in the twentieth century (Collier 1988). Originally affiliated with the Confederación Nacional Campesina (CNC) in order to obtain routes by which Zinacantecos could legally transport their produce to market without competition, the transport unions experienced the PRI's political cooperation. One union, for example, did not receive authorization from transport authorities until its leader, an activist in the then-opposition Partido de Acción Nacional (PAN), abandoned his opposition to local PRI authorities by joining the PRI in the early 1980s. At that time, the organized truckers led the alliance of Zinacantán's PRI leaders with state authorities. This alliance deflected the opposition of dissident Zinacantecos (who affiliated with the PAN and the Partido Revolucionario Democrático [PRD]), keeping them out of power in Chiapas.

In contrast to shippers in the north, most of whom are neither unionized nor formally affiliated with producer groups, Zinacanteco truckers use their union membership to justify their transporting people as well as produce. In fact, although Zinacanteco truckers engage in wholesale produce trade on their own, they also serve other Zinacanteco producers by transporting them and their fruit, flowers, chickens, beans, and corn from the hamlets where they are grown to regional markets. Were truckers not organized as producers' transport unions, they would not be permitted to transport passengers legally, in competition with bus lines for example, without acquiring special licenses.

As producers' organizations, the Zinacanteco trucking unions thus monopolize and regulate the hauling of produce and passengers from Zinacantán along the routes linking the community to San Cristóbal de

Las Casas to the east and Tuxtla Gutiérrez to the west. No single truck works the Tuxtla–San Cristóbal route independently of the union. Union leaders set and strictly regulate the schedules on which member truckers operate their vehicles on a rotating basis to share both the profitable opportunity to haul loads and passengers on prime market days and the responsibility to work the route when the volume of traffic may not bring a profit. The first truck will leave a given hamlet around sometime after midnight in order to coordinate with departures of other trucks from other hamlets to provide regular service every forty-five minutes along the Pan American Highway between the region's major cities. Some of the trucks are specified to go into San Cristóbal, pick up cargo and passengers, and then head for Tuxtla. Others pick up passengers and cargo in the hamlets and depart directly for Tuxtla Gutiérrez. The union sets fares for passengers and freight, and imposes fines up to fifty thousand pesos for truckers who fail to keep to their schedule. Drivers adhere to the schedule even though many complain of the costs and unprofitability of working the market route on off days. Northern trucking, by contrast, ranges unregulated over the landscape at whatever pace and schedule the produce markets will bear.

Organizationally, Zinacanteco trucking appears to spread opportunity and costs among truckers, more as a way of sharing burdens and responsibilities than explicitly as a way of limiting risk. In contrast, northern entrepreneurs accept high risk and cutthroat competition. In fact, northern *fruteros* actually take advantage of market fluctuation as part of their entrepreneurial strategy; for example, they may, at considerable risk, buy more than they can sell immediately so as to speculate on anticipated changes in the price or supply of a product that might bring a windfall profit. By contrast, the Mayas buy and sell produce in ways calculated to share burdens and opportunities rather than simply to circumvent risk. Zinacanteco truckers adhere to union rules to apportion to one another as clients the Maya buyers and sellers whom they serve. Truckers ship wholesale only for specific and regular clients, who in turn sell flowers in specified amounts.

Zinacantecos plan their market transactions with great specificity and care in part because they have limited capital at their disposal. In contrast to northern shippers, who can obtain merchandise on credit and who use credit as a major commodity in almost every transaction, Zinacantecos have limited access to credit outside their community and must make virtually all of their wholesale transactions on a cash basis. Produce merchants carefully harbor their capital, calculating how much to invest and spend in each transaction without taking undue risk. They are not willing to speculate in the products that they ship and trade.[6]

At the same time, the truckers characteristically are themselves involved in farming and marketing in which they can use their vehicles strategically. Most drivers do not expect to make big profits in transport alone. Instead, they see trucking as an adjunct to farming. As farmers, they need money to buy fertilizer and herbicides. They need to ship fertilizer to the field and corn to market.[7] By hauling fare-paying passengers and produce with their own farm investments and harvest, they can generate cash flow and minimize their own transport costs.

The care with which Zinacantecos manage wholesale buying and selling is embedded in complex cooperative trading arrangements that parallel the organized operation of trucking by the Zinacanteco unions. Unlike northern entrepreneurs who compete individually, groups of Zinacantecos band together to undertake the selling and buying of flowers. Interviewing truckers and flower merchants who supply the markets of Tuxtla Gutiérrez, for example, we learned of groups of six to eight *socios* (partners) who work together selling flowers at a given *puesto* or market stall. Members of such a group work together to package bulk goods obtained from local producers and to ship produce to market, even though each may purchase his produce separately. Then, each day, one of the group will travel to Tuxtla to sell. This rotates use of the stall among members of the group, both providing access to the market and sharing the burden of fixed expenses. Meanwhile, individual members have time to maintain their milpa according to the season.

Trips to Mexico City to purchase flowers also use group organization to pool capital, spread costs, and share risks. The group contracts for a trucker and driver to make the trip, usually on a regular basis, pooling and sharing the costs of freight and expenses. For such trips to be profitable, the trucks must be fully loaded on the return trip. No single individual can afford or market the volume needed to fill a truck. One long-haul trucker we interviewed regularly took six individuals to buy flowers wholesale in Mexico City to fill his eight-ton truck, each in turn representing a different group of vendors. As a result of this and other similar arrangements, large numbers of vendors essentially share the costs and risks of the long-haul wholesale business in flowers, minimizing any given vendor's competitive advantage.

Vendor groups rotate among their members the responsibility of accompanying the trucker to Mexico City to buy flowers in the Central de Abastos. This rotation generalizes both knowledge of the product and skills to buy. Mario Chofer, a driver of an eight-ton truck that travels to Mexico City weekly for one consortium, gave us a description of a typical run, which we summarize:

Six *comerciantes* go on each trip, leaving Tuesday morning. Two ride in *la cabina* and the rest in the *plataforma* (back). They take turns riding in the front. The first two ride to Matías Romero, Oaxaca, the next two until Córdoba, and so on. They get to the Mexico City market around 3 a.m. Wednesday, and they all sleep. Around 6 a.m. the *comerciantes* begin their buying, asking prices for tube roses, chrysanthemums, gladioli, and such. This goes on until about 8 a.m., when Mario awakens and checks over the truck. By then the *comerciantes* are getting their flowers ready and begin loading the truck. He eats and they load until about 10 or 10:30 a.m. Once on the road, the *comerciantes* take turns in the cabin, *platicando* (conversing) to keep Mario awake. They arrive around 6 or 7 a.m. Thursday in Tuxtla Gutiérrez, where the *revendedores* (resellers) are already awaiting them at the Ancianos market. The truck also makes stops at the Mercado Nuevo and the San Juan markets in Tuxtla, and in Chiapa de Corzo and San Cristóbal. Mario reaches San Cristóbal by around 9:30 a.m. and he returns to his hamlet in the afternoon.

A given trip takes about forty-eight hours and is usually scheduled once per week by a vendor-trucker consortium. Once established, this relationship between driver-trucker and buyers remains stable and predictable. This managed sharing of burdens and responsibilities to secure predictability may be comparable to collective bargaining in its economic consequences. Under arrangements of collective bargaining, productive enterprises tend either to swim or to sink all together, doomed if conditioning economic factors pass some threshold. For example, when Zinacanteco minibus drivers from one hamlet, Navenchauk, tried to raise their fares to meet rising fuel costs early in 1992, others of Zinacantán refused to authorize the fares or to patronize them, and this group of entrepreneurs went out of business.

Zinacanteco trucking differs from northern trucking not only in its corporative management and studied predictability, but in the way political power uses and shapes it much more than in the north. The "policing" of routes and schedules by union leadership helps ethnic leaders to effect political control of compatriots even as Zinacantecos expand the scope and range of their livelihoods outside the domains over which ethnic leaders once held power. Energy development during the 1970s and into the early 1980s afforded Zinacantecos a degree of "career mobility" of the kind Richard Adams (1970) wrote about as circumventing the power of ethnic brokers. In the retrenchment that followed the 1982 debt crisis, brokers reasserted control, albeit over new or expanded domains. In the case of trucking, Zinacanteco leaders struck deals with transport authorities to monopolize routes of supposed "peasant" transport of both cargo and passengers. The unions became the mechanisms for truckers to obtain the license plates they needed to haul both "producers" and their "products" to market on routes that compete with regional bus lines. Without these plates, drivers would have been limited to *servicio particular*, or noncommercial transport, eliminating the possibility of fare-paying passengers. Union truckers put up with the policing of their schedules because their presidents have the power to grant or remove the licenses on which their businesses depend. For their part, the union presidents work closely with transport authorities on all sorts of regulation, legal and extralegal, of member truckers. Such exercise of political power in trucking organization is less apparent in the north, where truckers long have enjoyed the relatively unregulated freedom of the *ruta abierta* ("open road," or route without fiscal check-points) and are at most subject to the more veiled control exercised by entrepreneurial patrons over their trucker clients.

The politics of trucking extends into Zinacanteco life more gener-ally than it does into the lives of northern truckers because the dominant political faction of Zinacantán, affiliated with the PRI, is identified with the truckers. The so-called *Camioneros* (truck owners) have managed to work out accords among themselves and with state authorities that con-tribute to their control of positions of public leadership, especially in civil posts of the *cabecera's* (district's) town hall, but also in the cargo sys-tem of ritual positions centered in the *cabecera*. In the 1988 presidential elections, the Camioneros held sway over other Zinacanteco factions, including so-called *Campesinos* (peasants), who sought support from out-side the then-ruling party (the PRI) by affiliating with the PAN or the PRD. In popular class terms, Zinacantecos see the trucker as glamorous but also as involved in the exercise of power that some argue is self-interested rather than in service of the ethnic community. At the same time, many of the opposition are Zinacanteco *comerciantes* who depend on the truckers to haul their flowers and other produce.

The Organization of the Produce Trade as Ethnic Enterprise

The fact that Zinacanteco truckers have organized into unions ostensi-bly as peasants who need to transport their produce to market helps truckers justify their claims that they are providing a service to their community—a self-justification that northern shippers do not make. Zinacanteco truckers tell stories of the old times, in which Maya of the highlands of Chiapas carried loads on tumplines, as times when Indians were reluctant to use what motor transport there was because ladino truckers would mistreat or cheat them. Now, truckers say, fellow Zina-cantecos can transport their produce to market reliably and without the exploitation that they might otherwise experience as ethnic people of the region.[8] Many Zinacantecos who do not speak Spanish—especially women—are willing to venture into the commercial world that Tzotzil-speaking truckers open up to their ethnic compatriots. Truckers thus redefine and expand the domain in which Mayas can conduct their lives as ethnic people.

Indeed, the ethnic specialization of regional marketing, which also distinguishes Zinacanteco shipping from that of the north, began in earnest when transport came under Maya control, enabling Zinacantecos to penetrate markets to which they lacked access either as strangers or because of want of product to vend. Zinacanteco flower selling, which had begun on a limited scale in the 1960s (Bunnin 1963), spread through the region only after Zinacanteco trucking augmented the supply of flowers by facilitating wholesale purchases from Oaxaca and central Mexico. The truckers assure supplies of flowers even when given varieties are out of season in Chiapas. They also assure trustworthy transport from Zinacantán to regional markets. As a result, Zinacantecos now sell flowers on a regular basis in scores of small market stalls in towns throughout Chiapas. And although other Mayas of the region also sell produce, the specialization in flowers has remained Zinacanteco.

The groups into which Maya *comerciantes* band as *socios* also encourage fellow Mayas to venture into the market world of Mexican nationals as individuals, either as common citizens or as Mayas. In fact, although trading groups make up a significant part of the Zinacanteco produce trade, many Zinacantecos undertake such commerce as individuals. Some are Zinacantecos who pioneered in flower trading long ago, and who now own and run the largest independent *puestos* with their own employees. But there are also scores of individual Zinacantecos who sell produce on just an occasional basis, on the curbside at the margins of markets rather than at a market stall.

Among these curbside vendors are women, many of whom speak little or no Spanish, who now dare to venture into markets. Such occasional vendors are helped out by being able to turn to compatriots among the organized Zinacanteco *comerciantes* for advice and protection in an alien world. Carol Smith (n.d.) has pointed out that Maya women in Guatemala move most freely within their ethnic communities and are, conversely, circumscribed in their economic and social possibilities outside community bounds. She theorizes that ethnicity gives Guatemalan

Maya women relative autonomy and personal security within their communities in exchange for forgoing marriage outside the community. For Maya women in Chiapas as well, ethnic communities are domains that afford protection as well as freedom of movement. Zinacanteco truckers, in effect, are expanding the territorial boundaries of "community" within which their women can move about, seek redress for wrongs, and be reasonably assured of security and appropriate social and sexual conduct. It is as though Zinacanteco shippers and truckers have extended the domain of the ethnic community into the world of Mexican nationals without giving up their ethnicity.

Traversing the Borderlands in Ethnic Enterprise: The Strategic Role of Trucking

We have described and compared two situations, in Mexico's northern and southern borderlands, in which ethnically disadvantaged trucker entrepreneurs from less-developed domains nonetheless trade in the wealthier, dominant society to their north. In our comparison of northern and southern Mexican trucking, we have attempted to make a contribution to a comparative study of trucking borderlands as constitutive of heightened ethnic enterprise. In the north, truckers (re)create ethnicity as the use of patronage, reciprocity, and trust to ameliorate competitive individualism. In the south, they expand the reach of the politically constructed domain of collective ethnic enterprise.

In part, we have characterized the expansion of Mexican trucking culture in relation to the spread of communication across the frontier that once isolated southeastern Mexico from the center and the north. As trucking burgeoned in the south, highland Maya truckers embraced much of the popular culture of trucking, donning *norteño* attire— "Texan" hats, boots, and clothes—while on the road, even as they doff it in favor of their own ethnic garb when at home. Behind the image that both sets of truckers project, we nonetheless identify sharp differences in the entrepreneurial styles and organization with which truckers undertake their businesses. Northern truckers employ elaborate interpersonal networks of reciprocal obligation, *confianza*, and patronage in the organization of highly competitive northern transport. Highland Mayas draw on a cultural repertory of more corporatist organization to secure ongoing transport and produce businesses in an economic context that will not sustain the heavy traffic of the north. In each case, we relate characteristics of style to the context and history within which truckers have elaborated them. Trucking cultures thus deserve study as ways in which people formulate styles of being ethnic as the basis of mobilization vis-à-vis others (Williams 1989, 1991), whether within a given nation or in the transnational context of offshore production, restructuring, and free-trade agreements.

When truckers venture into new and alien domains, they seem to attain a foothold in popular class enterprise that is segmented from other transport and produce trade in a manner that invites comparison to relationships of informal to formal sectors more generally. Informal production situates sweatshops, cottage industries, and piecework distinctly from formal workplaces. Analogously, Zinacanteco truckers developed distinctive routes as they began to deliver flowers and produce for small-scale vending at the edges of regional markets. Mexican produce traders took over Los Angeles's Seventh Street Market as dominant sector traders vacated the market in favor of the newer and larger Los Angeles Wholesale Terminal facilities. Heretofore, informal sectors have been studied most frequently with respect to their exploitation of labor (see, for example, Sassen-Koob 1983) and with respect to their tapping and reconfiguring of personhoods and gender for extraction of surplus (Fernández-Kelly 1983). The "implosion of the Third World into the first" (Rosaldo 1985) and "peripheralization at the core" (Sassen-Koob 1982) involve more than the migration of popular-class people into the borderlands and their production of ethnic identity there as exploited proletarian labor (Rouse 1991; Kearney 1988).[9] We suggest that informal sectors also deserve study in relation to their popular-class entrepreneurial businesses, such as trucking and produce trade, understood in terms of their culturally mediated styles of exploitation and relation to dominant sectors.

We have seen that Maya truckers reconfigure the space in which their compatriots, men and women, may conduct petty commerce, effectively extending the ethnic community into formerly alien markets and extending the scope, range, and meaning of the ethnic community. Northern truckers, analogously, have reconfigured the Los Angeles wholesale produce markets for their compatriots as ethnically differentiated places. Despite their different circumstances and style, both truckers of northern Mexico and their highland Maya counterparts of the south have expanded their enterprises into the alien domains of their respective borderlands. Each group has had to confront not just the risks or uncertainties that attend any business expansion, but the disadvantages as well of having to penetrate foreign turf where others' cultural styles dominate. Each has built on earlier contacts and knowledge of the markets they entered, highland Mayas having formerly sold corn into regional markets and the northern *comerciantes* having had prior links to Los Angeles and other U.S. markets. Each has secured a definitive and singular presence in alien territory by elaborating a distinctive cultural style of entrepreneurial organization. Each has traversed the borderlands in trucking, which in itself is productive of intensified ethnic enterprise and of expanded meanings for ethnic communities of a kind that will probably become more apparent, rather than less so, in the years to come.

CHAPTER 4

The Transnational Market:
The Case of Los Angeles

The Los Angeles Wholesale Terminal (LAWT) is one of the largest produce centers in the United States, and one of the largest in the world. The market's importance lies not in its size, however, but in its role as a hub of transnationality. The market includes commodities that arrive from every corner of the world. It mirrors a deep ethnic complexity connected to specific types of produce and their places of origin throughout the world. As is the case in many wholesale terminal markets throughout the United States, ethnic entrepreneurs have been instrumental to the rise of the produce trade in Los Angeles commerce.

Many U.S. wholesale produce markets began in designated areas of major cities where ethnic neighborhoods and new immigrants sought harbor. The Essex Street market of New York's Lower East Side is perhaps the best example. Viewed from this perspective, these market hubs are long-standing centers of transnationalism and global enterprise.

The LAWT exhibits both economic and sociocultural behavior that is often believed to be simply a border phenomenon. This chapter discusses the complex hierarchy of Mexican participation in the LAWT, drawing attention to the various strands of accommodation of recent and long-standing personnel that are connected to the market. Commercial activity and its supporting labor in the LAWT have long been connected to the entrepreneurial activity of Mexicans, Mexican production regions, and Mexican markets south of the border. Following the various ebbs of immigrant *entradas* into the United States, Mexican entrepreneurs followed and introduced commodities that became market staples over the years, producing regional traditions of labor and commercial activity tied to specific areas of crop production. Since the early 1990s, the LAWT has become increasingly diversified in the type of commodities it distributes, mirroring the changing demographics in California and throughout the United States.

The specific structure of the market and its composition reflect the hierarchical accommodation of new ethnicities to the United States. The role of Mexican-origin entrepreneurs and labor has especially intensified. This is the result of both historical and sociocultural patterns of transnationality between the United States and Mexico, producing social patterns that "cross" the border but are sustained in market activity. When viewed from a transnational lens, the LAWT is part of a broader entity—an encompassing U.S.–Mexican transnationality in which commodities, immigration, and entrepreneurial activity are tied together. The "business" of Mexican commodities at the LAWT has been engendered by the transnational circuits traveled by Mexican-origin entrepreneurs.

Between 1984 and 1989, I worked in the produce industry and observed and participated in the exchange of Mexican commodities in both Mexico and the United States, primarily in the city of Los Angeles. I worked in the LAWT as a representative of a Mexican chile pepper packinghouse and distributor located on the border in Tijuana, Baja California. I was responsible for sales and distribution of Mexican-grown chile peppers and other fresh Mexican produce commodities in Los Angeles. This activity offered me firsthand contacts with other distributors and wholesalers. The analysis in this chapter is based on participant observation and interviews conducted with the heads of Mexican produce departments, owners of produce businesses, and distributors in both Los Angeles and Tijuana.

Mexican and Mexican-American entrepreneurs control the distribution of Mexican fruit and commodities in the city of Los Angeles. Mexicans buy fruit in Mexico and sell and distribute it in both the wholesale markets in Los Angeles and to retailers who sell in Mexican neighborhoods throughout the city. Mexican immigrant entrepreneurs and a Mexican workforce form a major portion of the daily activity of the industry.

The hierarchical structure of the Los Angeles market illustrates a corresponding hierarchical adaptation of immigrants into differing layers of market activity. Yet market control rests on both capital and knowledge of distribution channels, primarily in Mexico. Without such knowledge, even the economically richest produce houses and entrepreneurs in the United States would not survive. Mexicans take advantage of knowledge from home regions about specific commodities in demand among immigrants and native Mexican-Americans, as part of their integration into the economy of Los Angeles.

The massive migration of Mexicans into the United States is commonly viewed as being composed primarily of the undocumented who participate in peripheral sectors of the economy. The closeness of the border, economic disparities, and high unemployment in Mexico all contribute to a cyclical flow of secondary labor into the United States. Viewed from an international perspective, in which immigrants are strategically taking advantage of the international demand for commodities in both Mexico and the United States, and in conjunction with the intense population density of Mexicans, the Los Angeles experience points to the existence of a highly ethnic business community, of consumers and workers who are part of a broader hemispheric system in the fruit and vegetable business. Entrepreneurial activity thrives because of continuing mass arrivals from the home country, providing immigrant entrepreneurs with privileged access to sources of low-wage labor and new consumer markets. Immigrants in the enclave, in turn, take advantage of language and cultural affinities. Reciprocal obligations in a common ethnicity create opportunities for new kinds of businesses and new patterns of mobility for immigrant workers. In addition, economic expansion enables immigrant entrepreneurs to capitalize on past investments in human capital (Portes and Bach 1985, 203).

There has been very little investigation of Mexican immigrant entrepreneurs and their roles in the U.S. economy. This is surprising given the scale and history of Mexican immigration to the United States, but is owing, at least in part, to the focus of research and public attention on immigration policy, health and social-service usage, settlement, and the undocumented worker. In large cities, the Mexican immigrant and the undocumented worker are very visible in the service industries (restaurants and hotels), agriculture, and small industries surrounding the city. Mexican neighborhoods are full of consumers and workers of Mexican origin (Mexican-Americans and Mexican immigrants), but the literature generally paints these communities in broad strokes in such a way as to occlude immigrant entrepreneurs. Although one study on enterprises in Mexican-American neighborhoods focuses on the perceptions of Mexican immigrant workers and sheds important light on the entrepreneurial behavior of Mexicans and Mexican-Americans (Hansen and Cardenas 1988), there are few specific studies of Mexican entrepreneurs in urban centers of the United States. George Sanchez (1993) does provide a thorough background of the early history of Mexican entrepreneurs in Los Angeles.

The Los Angeles Wholesale Produce Market: The Setting

Los Angeles contains one of the largest wholesale produce markets in the world. The city's produce industry consists of three main markets: the Olympic Street Market (the official Los Angeles Wholesale Terminal), the Seventh Street Market, and the Ninth Street or City Market. The Olympic Street Market opened in 1986, covering approximately forty acres of new buildings and parking areas for clients loading and unloading produce. The other two markets, each a full square city block, were once the heart of the Los Angeles produce industry, but now only complement the new wholesale market.

Between 1986 and 1989, as larger and better-established distributors moved into the new market, stalls in the other two markets were taken over by newcomers. Vacated stalls in the City Market, commonly known as the Ninth Street Market, were initially rented by Korean and other Asian immigrants. They featured a high concentration of Asian produce (although other vendors of all merchandise are present). The Seventh Street Market stalls were filled mainly by Mexican-origin entrepreneurs, many of whom were first-generation immigrants, leading to its transformation into a primarily Mexican commodity market.

Los Angeles is known for its high-volume business in Mexican produce and commodities. Primarily as a result of immigration from Mexico, Los Angeles's Latino population increased 57.3 percent in the decade between 1970 and 1980, compared to an increase of only 5.5 percent in the city's total population (Light and Bonacich 1988, 4). This trend continues. Of the 9,500,000 individuals estimated by the 2000 U.S. Census to reside in Los Angeles County, some 4,200,000 were of Hispanic origin. A high percentage (71 percent) of this 4 million were Mexican. The continuing growth of the Mexican population will increase not only the number of entrepreneurial activities of Mexicans, but also the "built-in" market for Mexican commodities.

This demand for Mexican commodities has created a very competitive market in the city. In the past, small retailers located in the Mexican heartland of East Los Angeles were the only handlers of Mexican produce and commodities. Today, however, not only do large chain stores boast Mexican departments, but entire supermarkets are dedicated to Mexican clientele, such as the Tianguis Super Markets of the Von's chain. These stores specialize in Mexican produce and groceries. Chorizo counters, huge meat departments featuring Mexican cuts, *panaderías* selling fresh-baked sweet bread and tortillas, and even mariachi bands attract Mexican customers. These markets are strategically placed in the Mexican neighborhoods around the city.

As demand grows and retail competition for control of clientele continues, a parallel growth in wholesale activity permeates the produce industry. Mexican satellite markets have developed around the main Olympic and Seventh Street terminals to meet the demand to which the large chain stores have yet to respond. Whereas the larger firms from the main markets cater to the large chain stores and other large-volume clients, the satellite markets cater to smaller retailers who sell Mexican products in neighborhood stores or to street vendors who sell from fruit trucks and vans. These satellite markets include the Central Street Market, the Casa Blanca, the Overland Terminal Warehouse, and La Amargura.

The unifying characteristic of all these markets is their ethnic concentration. This includes the Mexican immigrants and Mexican-Americans in the main markets as well as the small entrepreneurs in the satellite markets. The commodity being sold, the workforce, the business population, and the clientele are all mostly of Mexican origin.

The high demand for Mexican commodities and produce in Los Angeles has contributed to the establishment of a high ethnic concentration of Mexican entrepreneurs and a Mexican workforce in the city's produce industry. The economic activity of this population is geographically centered in the city's produce market terminals. All of these markets, both central and satellite, are concentrated within a two- to three-mile radius. This concentration of ethnicity is an important aspect of economic exchange throughout the market system. Mexican entrepreneurs depend on their Mexican clientele and workforce, and newcomers to the industry depend on opportunities in the Mexican-owned and -operated businesses.

The Market Hierarchy

Anthropologists have studied the behavior of small entrepreneurs in produce markets in the United States, but their work has focused on decision making in marketplaces (e.g., Plattner 1982, 1984, 1985b; Byrne 1985). Anthropologists working in societies that have highly organized and complex markets, however, have focused on the functional hierarchies of markets in central places. Most of this work has been in agrarian societies, but the hierarchical concept borrowed from central place theory, developed by G. William Skinner, has been applied to urban markets as well (Smith 1985). Although this model has yet to be applied to urban market settings in the United States, the concept of a hierarchically structured market illuminates the functions of differing entrepreneurs within the Mexican market of Los Angeles.

The hierarchical levels of the Los Angeles Mexican market parallel both the different modes of incorporation and the immigrant status of the Mexican-origin population in the market economy. The incorporation of this population into the wholesale produce market closely mirrors descriptions of immigrant incorporation into the primary and secondary labor market generally. Simply put, native-born citizens (i.e., Mexican-Americans) are situated in the best job positions. There are some immigrants, however, who are longtime U.S. residents and who have experience in the Mexican market. These individuals own businesses or work in prestigious wholesale houses as salespeople. On the other end of the scale are the small entrepreneurs who buy and sell on a small scale at the satellite markets, and peddle their produce on community routes throughout the city. Although these entrepreneurs face a constant threat of economic failure, there is also the possibility of advancement into other levels of the market hierarchy.

In addition to the entrepreneurs who work within the Mexican market structure, there is also a labor force composed primarily of Mexican-origin immigrants. This labor force is also tied into the market structure. The lowest-paying jobs with the least security at the lowest levels are filled by the newest immigrants. The most secure and higher-paying jobs are taken by long-term residents and native Mexican-Americans. Advancement in the hierarchy is possible. Various individuals serve as examples and role models. They began in low-level entry jobs and now fill prestigious and high-paying jobs in the large wholesale houses of the Los Angeles Wholesale Terminal.

This hierarchical structure of jobs and occupations is an important characteristic of the Mexican market enclave. Like the Cuban experience in Miami, the hierarchy provides occupational heterogeneity and a variety of opportunities for advancement in the market structure. Although this case is somewhat different than other enclaves because it is industry-specific, the variety of entrepreneurial activities and opportunities in the workforce are inducements for immigrant entrance. Furthermore, the high level of ethnic concentration encourages Mexicans to seek jobs and opportunities among ethnic peers in a familiar cultural environment. Individuals who do business in all levels of the market structure depend on the Spanish language and transactions generally follow economic customs specific to Mexican *fruteros*.

The Olympic Street Market

The Olympic Street Market, officially known as the Los Angeles Wholesale Terminal, houses the largest wholesale establishments and is the most prestigious of the markets. The firms here handle high volumes of commodities, have stable financing, and deal with sales on a credit basis. These businesses are listed in the produce industry "blue book," the so-called bible of the industry. In addition to its descriptions of the uniform commercial code to govern sales and the Perishable Agricultural Commodities Act , the blue book rates produce establishments on the basis of financial confidence, stability, and standards of pay practices (Produce Reporting Company 1988). Financial statements and produce industry reports on each business provide the evidence on which these ratings are based. Businesses throughout the country use the blue book ratings in evaluating transactions with new customers. The Olympic Street Market enterprises are all listed in the blue book, legitimating them in their industry. Many of these businesses are among the largest and most successful produce firms in the nation.

Within the industry, businesses are referred to as produce houses. A house is synonymous with firm and business, but the term usually refers only to the larger establishments in the industry. A produce house can, and usually does, have different departments, each of which is headed by a specialist who has extensive experience in the care, handling, and procurement of specific types of fruits and/or vegetables. Summer fruit departments specialize in peaches, plums, and other fruits. Other common specialties are tomato departments, "Oriental" vegetable departments, and, in Los Angeles, Mexican produce departments.

Although most of the twenty-seven houses in the market handle some Mexican produce, only a handful specialize in Mexican fruits and vegetables in addition to other commodities. These establishments are known as Mexican houses, regardless of ethnic ownership. Because these establishments carry and specialize in Mexican commodities, they naturally cater to a clientele of people of Mexican origin.

At the Olympic Street Market, only two of the twenty-seven houses are owned by Mexican-origin businessmen. These businesses have been in operation for more than two decades and have established themselves as permanent houses. Both of these businesses are owned by Mexican-Americans who were born in the United States. Like many of the produce businesses, these houses had their start through single entrepreneurs who were able to advance, accumulate capital, and eventually own larger establishments. The owners of these houses are considered the "dons" of the Mexican market because, as small entrepreneurs who entered the market with no capital, they worked their way up and slowly built strong competitive businesses. They come from immigrant backgrounds and built their businesses through personal initiative and resources. As such, they are living examples of the possibility of advancement and long-range security in the market hierarchy.

Although these houses cater to Mexican clients, they also have special fruit and vegetable departments. The larger of the two houses has a strong department that caters to Korean and Chinese clientele. Both, however, have large "Mexican" departments in which Mexican produce is handled. This includes chile peppers, tomatillos, cilantro, jícama, Mexican white onions, nopales (cactus), tuna (prickly pear), chayote, tamarind, tamale leaves, fresh (drinking and mature) coconut, and other specialty items such as maguey hearts. However, the primary Mexican item is chile peppers (including jalapeño, serrano, güero [yellow hots], California green [Anaheim], and pasilla). These establishments sell great quantities of produce, as many as ten truck lots (trailer loads) a week of single items. One buyer-seller from a prestigious Olympic Street house reported using two full semitrailer loads of chile peppers a day to supply his customers. This is an average of fifty to seventy thousand pounds of fresh chile peppers a day.

This volume of business requires a number of diversified jobs, which are ranked in order of importance and income. The most prestigious position throughout the Los Angeles market complex (at all levels) is the salesperson, who is also the head of the department. Salespeople are powerful individuals because they have the backing and trust (to a certain extent) of the company to control purchases. They are seen as the ones that keep operations going. They "move" products (an important factor in perishable commodities) by controlling sales. Salespeople in the Mexican departments are mostly of Mexican origin. Out of the twenty-seven establishments in the Olympic Street Market, eight (in 1989) had Mexican departments, headed by salespeople of Mexican origin. Of these eight, however, the two Mexican houses were the strongest, handling the highest volume of product. Although other houses do not specialize in Mexican produce, they have departments that are also headed by Mexican salespersons.

There is one large establishment, located across the street from the main market, that is also considered part of the Olympic Street Market. Although not owned by ethnic businesspeople, this establishment boasts a huge warehouse of approximately fifty thousand square feet specifically for the handling of chile peppers and other Mexican products. The head salesman is not of Mexican origin, but is Latino, having grown up in Los Angeles in a traditionally Mexican neighborhood. Like other salesmen of the Olympic Street Market this man is bilingual. He began working in the Los Angeles market when he was fourteen as a chile sorter, then moved into loading and unloading, and finally became one of the most prestigious and powerful buyers in the Mexican commodity market. Like other buyer-sellers, he is a constant reminder and example of the possibility of advancement in the market hierarchy.

This stratum of owners (although few) and the prestigious salesmen of the Olympic Street Market represent the highest rung of the local produce hierarchy. They have the longest tenure in the industry and in the country. However, these individuals still maintain their cultural identity and foster ethnic concentration in the market.

A variety of jobs make up the occupation ladder in the Olympic Street Market. Mexican department crews vary in size. They are composed of aspiring sales assistants who are the right-hand "men" of the salesman, crew foremen who oversee the repacking and sorting of fruit, warehousemen who load and unload, and sorters who divide fruit into quality grades. Sorters hold the least prestigious jobs and are usually the lowest on the pay scale. Women are often employed as sorters, as this work requires no heavy lifting or use of large forklifts and dollies. Only men, however, can advance in this hierarchy of jobs and become salespersons. The workforce in this sector is almost entirely of Mexican origin.

Pay scales for these jobs show a great latitude. In 1989, sorters earned anywhere from minimum wage to six dollars per hour. Most loaders belonged to the Teamsters Union and earned eleven dollars per hour. Sales personnel, assistants, and foremen usually earn a salary. Salesmen earned as much as fifty thousand dollars a year and expected large bonuses. Some very prestigious salesmen secured personal use of a business car and enjoyed other privileges. One salesman, known for his skill in selling bananas, was responsible for the sale of more than fifteen loads (fifteen thousand cartons, equivalent to six hundred thousand pounds) per week. This man chose his own car and received bonuses often in excess of fifteen thousand dollars.

In addition to the regular employees of the produce houses, groups of men called "swampers" load and unload trucks on a piecework basis. Teams of men group around principal establishments and wait for truck arrivals. These teams are "contracted" to unload or load, and are paid set prices by the box, a sum that varies according to the different commodities. These are the most exploited of employees in the market. Jobs here are very tenuous, temporary, and insecure. The workers receive no health insurance or benefits of any type, unlike the regular jobs in the large establishments where benefits are often provided. These men are also the newest entrants into the market labor pool and often migrate from specific regions of Mexico.

The hierarchy of jobs exists in similar form throughout the market. Swampers, crew bosses, salespeople, sorters, and loaders are present in all the markets. The main difference is that in the smaller businesses these jobs are combined and often done by very small crews. In both the Seventh Street Market and the satellite markets, the salesperson, buyer, and crew boss are often the proprietor of the business.

Although many people enter the market in unskilled positions in the permanent labor force, the market structure provides differentiation and entrance into an entrepreneurial class. Market occupations at all levels are demanding (because of long workdays and abnormal hours), and businesses involve high risk (because of strong competition and the perishability of product), but the Mexican market often also provides alternatives not otherwise possible for new immigrants and others entering other segments of the labor force.

Each morning, there is a hustle and bustle of trucks, produce movement, and merchants hawking colorful fruits displayed under fluorescent lights as exotic and staple fruits and vegetables are sold, loaded, and carted away. The market business begins at 1 a.m. when crews arrive to set up fruit displays and orders for regular customers. Most houses open at 2 a.m. to begin deliveries and daily sales to merchants (both chain stores and others) who walk the market in search of quality produce, good prices, and to gauge the amount of fruit that entered the market that day.

The Olympic Street Market is the most prestigious and powerful of the market hierarchy. Although Mexican houses there are few, several major establishments have Mexican departments. The workforce is heavily Latino; one firm has more than a hundred employees, of whom 75 percent are Latino, mostly of Mexican origin. Throughout the market, Spanish is used on a daily basis in the majority of Mexican produce transactions. The Olympic Street Market exhibits a strong Mexican ambience that is accentuated by the use of the Spanish language, Mexican commodities, and the great number of ethnic personnel and clientele seen throughout.

The Seventh Street Market
The Seventh Street Market exhibits characteristics similar to the Olympic Street Market, but it is also different in many ways. The same type of produce is handled there and job types are similar. The main differences are the size of businesses and the more intense concentration of Mexican entrepreneurs, workforce, and clientele. The Seventh Street Market is largely a Mexican market. Although English is used in some transactions, the main language of proprietors, entrepreneurs, salespeople, and workers is Spanish. The number of businesses varies owing to a

high rate of failure resulting from foreclosures and the continuing entrance of new entrepreneurs who maintain businesses for short-term
periods. In 1988 there were thirty-six businesses in this market, of which
only ten did *not* specialize in Mexican commodities. Today, more than 90
percent of these businesses handle Mexican specialty items. Approximately seven of those that dealt in Mexican commodities competed with
the Olympic Street Market for customers. These seven were the largest
and better established houses on Seventh Street. Two of the larger
houses are branches of Olympic Street companies but are run as separate businesses. In addition, there are a number of small businesses run
by entrepreneurs who specialize in one or two commodities.

The head salesman of one of the larger firms (a branch of an
Olympic Street house) is Mexican-American, as is his assistant. Both
began their careers in produce markets under the tutelage of a famous
chilero. This man is said to have been the first to establish a chile pepper
business in the Los Angeles market, and subsequently became a proprietor of one of the Mexican houses on Olympic Street. Both of these men
worked their way up from being loaders and sorters, learned the tricks
of the trade, and finally landed jobs as salesmen. This particular firm is
the strongest on Seventh Street and handles high volume through the
long-established contacts and relations of the main salesman. In addition
to other Mexican commodities, this house imported at least one truck
lot (a trailer load) of chile per day (approximately twenty-five to thirty-
five thousand pounds, depending on the type of chile pepper). In high-
demand periods, this was doubled or even tripled. The other big house,
which is an Olympic Street branch, was headed by a Mexican salesman
who gained his permanent residency status through the amnesty of the
Immigration Reform and Control Act of 1986. For a period of two years
he was a salesman in the market while still an undocumented worker. He
is fully bilingual, having spent the majority of his adult life in the United
States. His assistant is Cuban. As in the Olympic Street Market, these
salesmen worked their way up the occupational ladder in the market.
Although they entered as basic laborers, they went on to hold prestigious and high-paying positions in the market hierarchy.

The Seventh Street Market is generally characterized by small Mexican entrepreneurs who depend on kin and other ethnic ties to compete. Of the newer entrepreneurs, González Brothers Produce (a pseudonym, as are other names used here) typifies the Mexican entrepreneur in the market. It is a family-run business. Three brothers, along with their father and a small crew of about five men, buy, sell, and conduct the entire business. Don Fernando, the father, started a small *frutería* (vegetable and fruit business) in Tijuana, the largest Mexican city along the U.S.–Mexican border of California. His sons worked and learned the business during their adolescence. As opportunities to sell Mexican products in Los Angeles increased, Don Fernando, like other Mexican *fruteros*, began crossing fruit into the United States. Ramón, the eldest son, soon realized that the opportunities for sales and profits were much greater in Los Angeles than in Mexico; but being on the market daily was necessary to gauge the flow of incoming fruit, prices, and the competition. Hence, Ramón and his brother Alfredo went to Los Angeles and opened a stall to receive produce that Don Fernando bought and sent to them from Tijuana. A third brother drives a small semitrailer tractor rig the family bought to control delivery and freight prices from Tijuana. After a two-year period on the Seventh Street Market, the González brothers were competing with Olympic Street and had grown from one stall to four. Ramón has established residency in Los Angeles, has learned English, and is considered a strong competitor in the market.

Several new businesses have entered the market, but have few permanent customers. One example of these is Sunny Boys Produce, in which two brothers and a cousin, along with a small crew of two or three men, buy and sell on a low-volume basis (one to three truck lots of produce a week). Their knowledge of the products, however, and their contacts in Mexico allow them to buy at good prices and remain competitive in the Seventh Street Market. Like the González brothers, the Sunny Boys got their start in Tijuana. They were relatively successful, but decided to move into the Los Angeles market when the Mexican peso collapsed. Their primary clients are the smaller entrepreneurs and retailers who trade in the market of the Overland Terminal, the Casa Blanca, and the Central Street Market.

The larger businesses of the Seventh Street Market approach the stability of the more secure firms in the Olympic Street Market. Seventh Street merchants, however, have less capital accumulation, less extensive credit (if any), and are unable to offer credit to other houses and merchants as the Olympic Street businesses do. Seventh Street merchants have smaller warehouses that do not allow the storage of large inventory. In addition, their inventory fluctuates, making regular and consistent sales to large customers very difficult. The most wanted customers, the large chain stores, customarily buy with the understanding that payment for purchases will be twenty-one days after sale, and often this turns into thirty days, which puts smaller merchants at a disadvantage. These sales tie up capital and disallow continued purchases and sales. The majority of merchants on Seventh Street rely on cash sales from most of their clients, enabling them to continue buying fresh produce and providing a slow accumulation of capital. They do establish regular customers, however, ideally a few preferred customers and occasional chain store purchases. These entrepreneurs capitalize on their contacts in Mexico and their knowledge about product sources and availability. These contacts often come from relatives or fictive kin, such as *compadres*.

José Ballesteros is a good example of a merchant who relies on these ties and social relations. He is the owner of one of the Seventh Street houses (Ballesteros Produce) that compete with the Olympic Street Market, has several strong customers, and occasionally sells to the chain stores. José specializes in the sale of chile peppers that he brings into the market through a *compadre* who buys the produce throughout Mexico. This contact and his ties to the chile trade in Mexico make José a strong competitor who is often sought out by larger houses to provide chile pepper when it is in short supply. José is a permanent resident who moved to Los Angeles with his family.

The Seventh Street Market hosts firms that are much less secure than the Olympic Street businesses. Wages for employees are generally lower, and most employees and proprietors do not have health insurance or other benefits. Most workers are not unionized. Although the possibility of advancement exists, such possibilities are fewer in these businesses than in the larger, more diversified houses in the Olympic Street Market.

What is significant in the hierarchy in the Seventh Street Market is the increased concentration of ethnicity and the dependence on ethnic and kin ties in conducting business. This market provides numerous opportunities for new immigrants arriving from Mexico. The fact that many Seventh Street entrepreneurs started as *fruterías* in Mexico serves as a link for newcomers who have had some experience in the fruit and vegetable trade in that country. In fact, many immigrants who work in the market as loaders and sorters arrived there through contacts among newly settled entrepreneurs. The Mexican market illustrates a privileged access to immigrant labor in which ethnicity and kinship are an important part of economic exchange. Furthermore, like the Olympic Street entrepreneurs and workforce, the Seventh Street Market is dependent on the initiative and resources of the immigrant ethnic population.

An important transnational characteristic is the unique history of these immigrants in the fresh fruit and vegetable industry in both Mexico and the United States. Unlike other Mexican immigrants entering the labor force, these immigrants arrive with specific skills and knowledge about Mexican produce that can be applied in adapting to the economy of the United States. Moreover, continued ties in Mexico serve to promote upward mobility in the economy and help create new opportunities. These immigrants utilize their past investments in social capital in the produce industry.

The Satellite Markets

The satellite markets are even more ethnically concentrated and have greater mutual reliance between immigrants and entrepreneurs than the Seventh or Olympic Street markets. The small entrepreneurs and merchants that surround the Olympic and Seventh Street markets operate within a two-tiered system. The most stable and economically secure merchants are those who rent and lease stalls in market buildings; the least secure and most vulnerable are the small entrepreneurs who sell from pickups and vans in Mexican neighborhoods throughout the city. The latter are called *sobreruedas* (literally "on wheels") in reference to their dependence on vehicles for sales and because they are always on the road. The satellite markets include the Central Street Market (a primarily Mexican market, although there is one Cuban business among eight permanent stalls), the Casa Blanca (an indoor market with five totally Mexican businesses), and the Overland Terminal Warehouse (within which are twenty separate Mexican-owned businesses housed in the main building). The satellite markets cater to a large group of small retailers who run neighborhood stores and the *sobreruedas*.

The Overland Terminal Warehouse resembles the produce markets throughout Mexico. Produce is stacked and displayed in the open, as individual vendors barter and negotiate prices and goods on a daily basis. A huge parking lot of approximately five acres turns into a bustling marketplace each morning, filled with 150 to 200 small produce vendors. These "vendors" own a van or small pickup truck that is converted for carrying fruit and vegetables, dry spices, chile peppers, and specialty items, such as Mexican candy, Mexican cassette recordings, and kitchenwares.

In addition to the buying entrepreneurs do in this market, another daily "market" caters to small vendors. This market is called La Amargura (The bitterness), because of the high competition and little satisfaction one gets in buying and selling there. La Amargura in many ways symbolizes the competition and daily struggles of the small entrepreneurs who enter the market. La Amargura represents the lowest tier of the hierarchy. "La Amargura" is located on Hemlock Street, directly across from Olympic Street and the Los Angeles Wholesale Terminal. This, I was told, is the "sal si puedes" (get out if you can) street of the Mexican market.

Although there are a few establishments outside of these markets on streets close to the Olympic and Seventh Street markets, they number less than a half a dozen and are dispersed rather than being clustered. Some forty-five establishments make up this final tier within the Central Street, Casa Blanca, Overland, and La Amargura markets. These businesses rarely purchase whole semitruck loads of fruit, as is more common in the Olympic and Seventh Street markets, but buy in volume based on pallets. Pallets are wooden flats on which boxes of produce are stacked for loading onto semitrailers. Each pallet takes an average of forty boxes of fruit (varying on the type of fruit), and a full semitruck averages sixteen pallets of merchandise.

The more financially stable *fruteros* will occasionally buy up to six pallets of single types of merchandise. They are more likely, however, to purchase three or four pallets. Three or four of these *fruteros* buy mainly from the Olympic and Seventh Street markets. Smaller merchants also buy from the larger markets on a smaller scale and usually pay cash for their purchases.

Fruteros who have established reputations as consistent buyers from the satellite markets are often extended credit on a short-term basis by both Olympic and Seventh Street houses. These individuals are referred to as "coyotes." This term refers to their alertness in buying and selling, their quickness to take advantage of situations, and their intense activity in the early-morning hours. Coyotes are allowed to select and take produce, but are not charged for it until the following day. Some coyotes are extended credit for up to three to five days. Collectors from the bigger establishments visit the coyotes on a daily basis, both to collect past-due amounts they are owed and to make arrangements for future sales. These are delicate dealings in which interpersonal relationships play a very important role. Business is done entirely in Spanish and is characterized by cordial joking relationships.

Establishments in the peripheral markets tend to be small family enterprises. Two or three people perform all tasks, including sales, sorting, packing, loading, and buying. Their hours are long and work is strenuous and difficult. These *fruteros* do their buying in the early morning hours between 2 and 4 a.m. They then return to their stalls to set up and begin selling to the small retailers and peddlers who buy between 5 and 7 a.m. Afternoons are spent sorting, repacking, and getting ready for the next day. These men often make buying trips to the fruit and vegetable markets in Tijuana. Besides the fresh Mexican produce (purchased in the Olympic and Seventh Street markets), these *fruteros* also buy other Mexican commodities such as dried chiles, condiments, candy, and housewares, which are resold in their stalls. They also sell some grocery items, such as canned chiles imported from Tijuana, tortillas, tamale leaves, and other Mexican specialty items. Although sales in the stalls are often on a retail basis, the main purchases are made by small retailers who will resell merchandise in neighborhood stores, or to the *fruteros* who drive vans and small trucks and peddle fruit in Latino neighborhoods.

Some *fruteros* also buy directly from Mexican distributors who buy products in Mexico and sell to the satellite markets. These distributors are a form of middleman, as they buy relatively large volumes and deliver goods to Los Angeles merchants. Most of them own one or two semitrailer-tractor rigs and employ a small crew of the most recent immigrants for unloading, sorting, and delivery. They rarely sell to the larger markets. On occasion, if a product is in high demand and availability is scarce, these distributor-haulers may be able to procure the product through contacts in Mexico and sell to the larger establishments. Juan Verduras is a good example of these distributors. He also illustrates the historical dimensions of the *frutero* in the Los Angeles market. A native of Jalisco, Juan was born, he says, into a family of the road: "Eramos de la carretera." His father and grandfather both hauled produce to nearby markets by *carreta*. He too took to the road and became a *trailero* (a driver of semitrailer-tractor rigs). His two brothers also took to the road and hauled, and his three sisters all married *traileros*. This was natural, says Juan, because most of their friends were *traileros*. At the age of eight, his father took him to Tijuana. Juan did odd jobs in the fruit markets there. He jokingly remembers crossing the border on a bicycle, buying and crossing two flats of tomatoes that he resold in Tijuana. He met his longtime mentor, Pablo, doing odd jobs in the vegetable market. Pablo took him in and showed him the trade. Juan accompanied Pablo on trips into San Diego County from Tijuana to assist in the buying and loading of avocados.

Working with this mentor, Juan was able to accumulate some capital and more experience. When Pablo bought a tractor rig, Juan took to driving long distances hauling fruit and vegetables throughout Mexico. "Entonces yo me subí" (That's when I climbed aboard), he says, referring to climbing aboard the tractor rigs to do long-distance hauling. This driving eventually led to hauling fruit into Los Angeles. As Juan accumulated capital and saw the opportunities of the fruit trade in the Los Angeles Mexican market, he decided to immigrate and bring his family to the United States. He lived initially in San Ysidro, but in 1989 moved to Los Angeles.

Juan's experience exemplifies the types of skills and historical circumstances that are unique to the *fruteros* who enter the Los Angeles market. He began learning the trade as a young boy in Mexico, and came from a family that was connected to commodity hauling for more than two generations. He received his training from a mentor who continues to be a major contact for product and business in Mexico. This experience made entering the U.S. market a natural step for Juan. The Mexican market offered a familiar cultural and economic environment in which he could remain independent, make a living, and advance in the market.

Juan subsequently focused on setting up his business in Los Angeles. Because of his success in hauling, he owns two semitrailer-tractor rigs, two refrigerated trailers, and is in partnership with a longtime friend, also a recent immigrant from Mexico. They specialize in buying and selling onions, and buy from as far north as Idaho. Juan is known throughout the market as a *cebollero*. During the winter months he focuses on the watermelon trade, buying in the Imperial Valley and in Mexico. In addition, he buys oranges directly from the packing sheds in Riverside, California. These are bought loose out of field bins rather than in packed boxes. He and a helper load the oranges onto a pickup truck converted to hold twice the amount of a normal pickup bed. Back in Los Angeles, a small crew of two men, both recent arrivals from Tijuana, unload and pack the fruit into standard cartons to be resold in the Mexican market. Unlike the packing sheds or the larger houses, there is no mechanization for packing.

Juan's reliance on his longtime friend, and the hiring of recent immigrants, illustrate another characteristic of this market that is common in other immigrant enclaves. The entrepreneurs rely on, and have privileged access to, immigrant labor that is entering the market. Like Juan, many of these immigrants come from agricultural regions in Mexico and have knowledge of the fruit and vegetable trade.

Juan has accumulated a few regular customers and is a stable buyer and seller. All his transactions are in cash. When he purchases a full load of merchandise, he pays on the spot. These purchases average around five thousand dollars but can be as high as ten thousand dollars or higher. In peak periods of the onion season, Juan buys up to five loads a week. Because of his attentive payments, he often gets preference over other buyers. He has a strong network of buyers and clientele throughout the market. His consistent buying and selling and his experience in Mexico and in Los Angeles have given him a foundation for his current business.

As a young man in his early thirties, Juan is typical of the *fruteros* who eventually enter the Seventh Street Market and compete with the stronger houses of Olympic Street. He continues doing his business in the Mexican market. He speaks very little English, and only rarely sells to Euro-Americans, but the bulk of his buying is done with non-Mexican growers. Juan is well known among the *fruteros* of the Mexican market. In addition to having met new *fruteros* in Los Angeles, he had worked with some of the Los Angeles *fruteros* in Mexico. This is not uncommon. In fact, one of the most successful of the *fruteros* at the Overland Terminal Warehouse is from Juan's home area in Jalisco.

The Open Market

The most insecure rung in this hierarchy is the open market, located in what was built as a parking area of the Overland Terminal Warehouse. Each morning 150 to 200 pickup trucks and vans converge on the area. Parked in parallel rows, these entrepreneurs begin the task of buying. *Fruteros* who have stalls in the warehouse building bring merchandise onto the lot in pallets, and other distributors park loaded trucks, selling directly from them. In all senses, this is an open market. These entrepreneurs buy by the box and fill their vehicles with a wide assortment of fruit and vegetables. In addition, tacos, burritos, sweet bread, coffee, and soft drinks are sold to the market vendors and clientele. Single vendors selling tamales and other foods roam throughout the market.

La Amargura is part of this open market, a ninety-yard street in which vendors park their trucks and sell directly to passing customers. Fifty to sixty merchants crowd onto the street. Although it is illegal to park and sell in this manner, it is done regularly. Occasionally, parking violations are given by police, but this results only in the merchants driving around the block and setting up shop again, as the police drive through the one-way street. These vendors are the newest entrepreneurs entering the Mexican market structure. They work on a day-to-day basis and have accumulated very little capital. Many of them regularly go back and forth to Tijuana, where they maintain their residences. The clientele of these *fruteros* are the small retailers and vendors who peddle their merchandise throughout the city in Mexican and other Latino neighborhoods. Because of intense competition, these small businesses are very vulnerable. In addition to being challenged by their peers, they face the increasing encroachment of the large chain-store conglomerates that are focusing on this ethnic trade.

This portrait of the Los Angeles market illustrates the rich contribution of Mexican entrepreneurs and labor to the city of Los Angeles, as well as the deep and complex transnationality that is played out every day. Although Los Angeles is some 120 miles from the U.S.–Mexico border, it is the presence of and connection to Mexican sociocultural systems that form the basis of the fruit trade. As part of a larger Mexican diaspora, *fruteros* illustrate the sociocultural attributes of a broader transnationality based on long-standing historical and social-cultural processes.

CHAPTER 5

Los Remexicanizados:
Mexicanidad, Changing Identity, and
Long-term Affiliation on the
U.S.–Mexico Border

I don't know how to put it in words, but to me it's an outstanding
feeling. And being a true Mexican. You know: I don't really like the
word Chicano. But it's alright. I think it's Mexican. Mexico. Viva
México. Y el chile atrás. Yeah, you feel proud of being a Mexican . . .
of your race. I think that's the way it should be. Even if you live here,
even if you were born here . . . you're a Mexican.

—Antonio Urcino Alvarez Castellanos

In December 1999, my great-uncle Tiburcio Castellanos passed away at
the age of ninety-three. Tiburcio, known as Tom by many and as Güero
by the family, was born in the small mining town of Julio César, now
long abandoned, just south of the U.S.–Mexico border in the territory
of Baja California. Tiburcio was the last of six children born to Cleofas
Gaxiola and Narcisso Castellanos. His birth took place in Mexico at the
insistence of his father, Don Narcisso, who with his wife and family had
previously trekked across the U.S.–Mexico boundary into the United
States and eventually settled in Lemon Grove, California.

Like Tiburcio, another son, Chicho (Narcisso), was born under similar circumstances. Cleofas once again returned to Mexico to give birth.
These boys, like the rest of the family, were born *mexicanos* but spent
their entire lives along the border in the United States. When Tom passed
away at ninety-three, he was still a Mexican citizen, though he spent only
four years of his life in Mexico (Mexicali), where he had attended grammar school and where he had met his wife, Refugio (aka Ruth).

Tom's life in the United States illustrates an accommodation to American society that exemplifies what social scientists call acculturation. He spoke fluent English, but never lost his Spanish, worked his way into a regular position as a skilled paint mixer, and retired from the Benson Paint Company in San Diego, California. His work at Benson Paint was deemed important to the national interest during World War II, so he was exempted from military service.

Tom was a good "citizen" known for his honesty, punctuality, and accountability. As a youth, he played baseball and learned to caddie and play golf at the Lemon Grove Golf Club, where he was the keeper of the greens. In short, he was a law-abiding person, an exemplary good "American" who contributed to and participated in U.S. society.

Tom Castellanos's life raises questions about the popular belief that in the long run, Mexicans, like other immigrant peoples, lose specific identities as they become assimilated into American society. Stories like Tom's are known throughout the U.S.–Mexico borderlands. Although born in Mexico, he was raised in the United States among a cohort of first-generation American citizens, many of whom, now octogenarians, continue to emphasize a certain "Mexicanness"—a *mexicanidad*—that contrasts sharply with sociological and anthropological predictions concerning the shedding of identities and gradual accommodation of immigrants to U.S. society and culture.

Curiously, some of these people, who have spent their entire lives in the United States, in the later stages of their lives have *reidentified* with Mexico and with being Mexican. These people grew up during an important period of U.S. history, the Great Depression, and they were tested patriotically in World War II. Yet, although they partook of and often immersed themselves in "American" life, they never lost their sense of identity as *mexicanos*. The numerous "Mexican-American" Veterans of Foreign War chapters, like the Don Diego Chapter in San Diego, and the strength of the GI Forum are good examples of the maintenance of this "ethnic" pride. (The GI Forum is an association of Mexican-American and Hispanic veterans of foreign wars dedicated to addressing problems of discrimination and inequities.)

Studies of Mexican immigration and settlement have focused on the slow accommodation/acculturation of Mexicans to life in the United States, yet few have examined the *reidentification* of border folk with previous national inclinations. It is assumed that most Mexicans who settle in the United States will eventually become Americanized—part of the sociocultural makeup of the country. Yet current border policy and contemporary political-economic realities are influencing and shaping new forms of identity for U.S. citizens of Mexican descent. For example, Chicanos and Chicanas, no longer stigmatized by Mexicans as *pochos* (half-Mexicans), are finding open arms in intellectual circles throughout Mexico; similarly, U.S. Mexicans range the border and interior of Mexico in newfound bicultural aptitude. The glory of Mexico beyond the border has captivated the cultural imagination, the desire for history, and curiosity about genealogy and the past for a new breed of people influenced by the presence not only of the border, but of Mexico, the neighbor nation-state. The border, the line in the sand, has influenced the many different kinds of recrossing that have taken place and made Mexico not just a nation for sojourning, but a place for reidentification. These border people are "returning" to Mexico, becoming *mexicanizados*, and expressing *mexicanidad*, regardless of having been born and having lived their adult lives in the United States.

Contrary to the acculturation model, the reidentification of U.S. citizens with Mexicanness is an important phenomenon that points to the diverse and eclectic nature of "borderlands" identities and questions the long-term model that ends with assimilation—partly a result of the scant studies, especially anthropological ethnographies, that have incorporated long-term ethnohistorical and sociological documentation of life on the border. The *longue durée*, with the analytical emphasis on the importance of changing social scenarios over time emphasized by Fernand Braudel in *On History* (1980), is hard to find in books about the border. In contrast, the observations in this chapter are based on long-term ethnographic work (and life) in a single community—Lemon Grove, California. As a native son, I first documented the entrance of pioneer migrants into this border town (see Alvarez, 1987), and over the past two decades have continued to document the history and life of my grand-parents' and parents' generations.

The "community" on which I focus is defined by the descendants of pioneer Mexican immigrants who settled in Lemon Grove. The town is now a unified city of more than twenty-three thousand people, just fifteen miles east of San Diego, approximately fifteen miles north of the U.S.–Mexico border. To most of Lemon Grove's residents, its history as an agricultural community and site of the first segregation court case in the United States is unknown. It was here that a group of Mexican immigrants challenged a 1930 school board decision to segregate the Mexican students of the public schools into a "Mexican" school for the instruction of English and Americanization studies. This case, named for my father—*Roberto Alvarez v. the Lemon Grove School Board*—has been documented in ethnography and film as an important precedent in Mexican-American history and in U.S. desegregation struggles (Alvarez 1986). The Mexican community, through the assistance of the Mexican consul, won the court case—the first school desegregation victory in the United States.

In the film *The Lemon Grove Incident*, there is a glorious finale in which justice prevails. The schoolchildren, numbering seventy-five first-generation American citizens, were allowed reentrance into the regular school. The popular consensus is that with this victory, these children were finally able to engage American life fully. This episode, it was believed, ensured a successful accommodation to society and to "being" American.

My work in the Lemon Grove community, however, illustrates a profound dissonance and marginality that prevailed during the years among first-generation Mexican-Americans following the court case, as well as with the succeeding generation, my own. These Mexican-American youths did indeed return to the "regular" school, but, ironically, they returned to segregated classrooms. The division of Mexican-American and Euro-American youth continued for at least the next twenty years. In a pattern that continues today, only 5 percent of these first-generation Mexican American children finished high school.

The Great Depression served both as an entry point for jobs in the greater American society and as an impetus to exploring the world out-side Lemon Grove. Young Mexican-American men and women worked in the Civilian Conservation Corps (CCC) and in the Works Progress Administration (WPA) of Franklin Roosevelt during the Depression. Later, most Mexican-American men patriotically signed up for the draft in World War II as infantry or navy personnel. The final outcome for the majority of the Mexican-American adults of this Lemon Grove gen-eration was an economic marginality, compared to the rest of their peers throughout the United States. Limited by education and a broader social-economic discrimination, only a minute percentage of this gener-ation was economically "successful." Most did not experience upward mobility, nor did they "succeed" in the American Dream.

The next Lemon Grove generation, my own, is sprinkled with com-plex social and cultural resonances that bespeak a period of both social marginality and changing identity. As this second generation matures (now past the half-century mark), the realization of a past seems to be reasserting itself—in Lemon Grove and other *mexicano* barrios in San Diego, on the border, and in Mexico. As one member of this second generation said, "At first we all wanted to be Americans because they [Anglos] didn't want us, so we fought like hell to prove that we were more American than even them. Now that we're older, that doesn't seem to matter. What's important is that we all want to be Mexicans."

This conflict and process in identity formation illustrates a pro-found contradiction in popular beliefs about acculturation and assimilation. The case of Lemon Grove not only challenges the broad-brush notion of "Americanization," but illustrates the unique variation of identity along the U.S.–Mexico border. Importantly, this also challenges assump-tions that it is the geographical border and the dual identity of both American and Mexican culture that influences a "borderland identity."

In at least one instance, it is Mexico, the neighbor nation-state, that incurs a "deep territorialization" and identification with specific locales and histories. It is an identity associated not with the border, but with Mexico. This identification invigorates identity tied to specific his-tory and place.

There is interesting evidence that the process of "Mexicanization" and the sentiment of being Mexican is not a solitary, isolated phenomenon. James Diego Vigil illustrates this process among Chicano high school students in Los Angeles (Vigil 1997). Vigil's study compares twenty-year educational achievement patterns among Mexican and Mexican-American high school students in two Los Angeles communities. He studied these neighborhoods first in the early 1970s, then returned in the late 1980s. He found sharp contrasts between the two periods. In the late 1960s and early 1970s, being "Mexican" was viewed by high school–age cohorts as a stigma to be shed. For these students, becoming "American" was the goal. During the late 1980s, however, high school cohorts in the same communities expressed a specific *mexicanidad*—an identification with being Mexican. They continued to strive for economic parity and class standing in "greater America," but being Mexican did not carry the stigma it did in the past. Of particular significance is that one of these cohorts is located outside of the barrio, in a second-generation suburban middle-class neighborhood.

Vigil's book is instructive because it deals specifically with American high school populations in Los Angeles. This ethnic identity was also recognized in a 1996 University of California Linguistic Report, which indicates that in Southern California a "Mexicanization" process has provided the Mexican-American population with a sense of pride and dignity in things ethnic or Mexican (McLaughlin 1993).

New social processes and identifications associated with ethnicity are not solely germane to California or the U.S.–Mexico borderlands. The cultural diasporas of new immigrant populations in Europe and throughout the United States indicate not a new "ethnicity," but a pronounced ethnic reidentification. Arjun Appadurai has eloquently discussed these phenomena in *Modernity at Large* (Appadurai 1996). Appadurai argues for the existence of a new social imagination expressed in our contemporary globalized world whereby the media, transportation, communication, and migration have come together in a manner that binds people to home communities in ways that were impossible in the past. Rather than being restricted because of territorial separation from homes, new (and old) immigrants are tied in novel and hybrid ways to their places of origin. With the contemporary advantage of the global media, transportation, and historical processes of immigration, people imagine and create new and different scenarios that are not tied to the bounded communities of the past. The multiple and regular instances of new immigrant enclaves throughout major U.S. cities that not only maintain but create new identities and ties to home regions and countries are a testament to this reassertion and reaccenting of national and ethnic pride.

For newcomers—first-generation immigrants the ethnic essence is always strong. But this sentiment, tied to ethnic identification, is expected to wither as time goes by, especially as these people become part of the American fabric. Lemon Grove, however, illustrates the perseverance of such ethnic sentiment and emphasizes the reconditioning and reengagement with ethnic identity based on a return and "reimagining" of ancestral ground—in this case, Mexico.

The *place* of the border is important here, because Lemon Grove is situated along the immediate borderlands with Mexico. Yet to the people of Lemon Grove, the reference is not the geopolitical line but the towns and places south of the border—Tijuana, Tecate, Ensenada—places that form part of a historical and present identity tying first-generation immigrants (parents) with current residents of San Diego County who are offspring and first- and second-generation U.S. citizens. The identification is not with a generic "Mexico" but with a Mexico that is made up of particular histories and memories, specific towns and individuals.

There has been an onslaught of redefinition in social-science literature aimed at addressing the contemporary processes of migration in globalism and transnationalism. This has been important in understanding current social processes in migration influenced by new technology and new forms of rapid transit and travel, media, and communication. It is the media, technology, and people's "imagining" new identities that spur new communities across geographic space, linking home and host societies in fundamentally new ways. Most of the immigration literature today not only outlines the settings to which migrants travel (as it did in the past) but also highlights original home communities. Such work illustrates the continuing connections and social-cultural processes that tie immigrants to new sites of settlement and to communities of origin. New terms that stress the overall processes of migrant agency, identity, and community stress the extensions of social processes across space and place, and are inclusive of home and host society in ways that often cross geopolitical boundaries such as the U.S.–Mexico border. Although these perspectives have been invaluable in redefining how social science (and anthropology in particular) have interpreted the process of migration and settlement, there has been little focus on the importance of place along the U.S.–Mexico border.

The border is continually presented as a place of social "hysteria," where individuals are confronted with multiple identities and conflicting nation-state prerogatives. Much of the popular literature links border identity, duality, and multiplicity in culture and language; it is the Mex-America of Carlos Fuentes (Fuentes 1986) and the Nine Nations of Joel Garreau (1981); it is an amalgamated mongrel that is constantly shifting. But for most of us who have lived this experience, the border offers more than the political-cultural divisions portrayed in much of the literature. There has been a dearth of work focusing on the actual agency (i.e., action) and praxis (i.e., practice) of individuals as knowers and agents of their own destiny in borderlands research. The border has come to be and to signify an oppressive structure controlled by the state and its agencies.

But there is also along the border a specific belonging, a "deep territorialization," that is connected not to the border as such, but to the communities, the histories, and the people that make up its social life. In describing the U.S.–Mexican border population, Carlos Vélez-Ibáñez states that "the border crossed us," essentializing the geographic-historical belonging of many border communities (Vélez-Ibáñez 1996). Donna K. Flynn, in "'We Are the Border,'" offers an apt contrast to the "deterritorializing" and "reterritorializing" of border people in the case of the Shabe on the Nigerian border—an appropriate comparison for communities of the U.S.–Mexico border (Flynn 1997). For the Shabe, as for Lemon Grove and other sites in the U.S.–Mexico borderlands, people express a sense of deep placement instead of displacement, a deep territorialization instead of deterritorialization. Such sense of place forges strong sentiments of rootedness in the borderlands themselves.

An important consideration in this regard is the variation of behavior in the U.S.–Mexico borderlands. The *interactions* of individuals in specific contexts create culturally significant behavior. It is precisely because people use (often strategically) their cultural identities that it is difficult for social scientists to identify what border folks "are." Border people are notorious for shifting and negotiating identities in social circumstances. There is a specific adherence to particular identities based on place, history, and belonging.

The people of Lemon Grove illustrate not just the pride of being Mexican, of being from the border, but the essence and process of "re*mexicanidad*." The essence of identity in their case is focused in the feeling of *being* Mexican. It is rooted in specific knowledge about specific persons, places, and histories tied to current realizations of ethnicity.

> It's something about being a Mexican, that you don't forget that you're a true Mexican. No le hace dónde naciste, even if you were born here in the United States from Mexican parents. You know you're Mexican. Nothing else. And not only that. You're proud of being a Mexican. No *chingaderas* [no screwing around]. It's one thing knowing, and not being one.[1]

Lemon Grove during the Depression and World War II was composed of a large working-class *mexicano* community that came mostly from the adjacent Mexican state of Baja California. Many of the settlers had come north via a mining circuit of booms and busts that led across the border into San Diego County. Lemon Grove provided a wealth of working-class jobs before and after the Depression in the lemon orchards, a citrus packing shed, and a gravel-mining quarry.

For most residents, and especially for the first-generation American-born, the Lemon Grove barrio was a safe haven where parents and *parientes* (relatives) made up the social world. Relatives often crossed into Mexico to Tijuana, Tecate, and Mexicali. In fact, many of the original settlers of Lemon Grove eventually returned to these Mexican border towns in the early 1930s, where they settled and remained. Family members fostered bonds with each other across the border through tightly woven extended families that shared a variety of important family affairs. Birthdays, baptisms, funerals, and weddings became events that helped the Mexican-Americans maintain ties to both sides of the geopolitical line. The picture painted by the surviving first U.S.-born generation is one of contentment and community cohesiveness, marked by the cultural identity of *mexicanidad*—fostered by their parents and the community—not of the border.

> Yeah, pues, casi toda la gente en Lemon Grove era puro unida as far as being Mexican. Yeah, I would say so. Yeah. Muy unida. Todo muy unido. Era muy importante vivir como un mexicano, pensar como un mexicano. We were all living here, al pie del cañón.

> Yeah, well, just about all the people in Lemon Grove were very united as far as being Mexican. Yeah, I would say so. Yeah. Very united. Always very united. It was very important to live like a Mexican, think like a Mexican. We were all living here, at the foot of the canyon.[2]

My father, Roberto R. Alvarez Castellanos, illustrates the essence of re-*mexicanidad*—a success story in social and economic terms, specifically through the accommodation of an American lifestyle. His life, however, illustrates a profound engagement with *mexicanidad*, especially during his later life. His story has meaning that goes beyond his success in American society.

Roberto Alvarez was chosen as a litigant for the school desegregation case. As a child, he spoke excellent English, did well in school, and was known as a punctual and diligent worker. He was the catcher for the local softball team, and in high school played football. During the Depression (and time of the school desegregation case), he and his brother and sisters held a number of odd jobs, contributing to the family's welfare. He worked at the local grocery store, cleaned chicken coops, and even tutored non-Mexican students. During World War II, he joined the U.S. Navy, learned bookkeeping, and served aboard ship in the Pacific. He was in Tokyo just after the surrender of the Japanese, and witnessed the ceremonial surrender of Japanese forces aboard his vessel. On his return from the Pacific, together with his cousin Henry Castellanos, he began a fruit distribution company with the money saved from previous jobs and the service. As the years went by, the business grew, and today, half a century later, it includes branches throughout California, Texas, and Mexico. Of special importance here is the essence of identity: first as a child, then later in the service, and as a businessman and entrepreneur, Roberto Alvarez was an exemplary "American." Yet, as the years went by, a certain Mexicanness flourished.

When my father was around sixty, he began frequent business sojourns into Mexico. These visits and interactions connected him with new and previous friends and relatives, influencing a rather dramatic celebration of *mexicanidad*. He always had fostered and maintained close relations with his extended family on both sides of the geopolitical border. His closest friends and allies were Mexican-Americans, but he moved gracefully in the Anglo business world. This strategic "American" profile was aimed at "success" in society. Because of the strong discrimination my sister Guadalupe had encountered in her first year of grammar school, my father insisted that we speak English at home—a break from many of the previous generation's insistence that Spanish be spoken at home. My father was intent on our survival and success in the American domain. He believed, practiced, and preached the American work ethic in which the individual is in control of his or her own destiny. The Mexicanness that was once restricted to interaction with *parientes*, friends, family, however, became a public symbol in both the United States and Mexico.

Roberto Alvarez was known as Don Roberto Alvarez throughout Mexican business domains. His regular dress included a broad-brimmed *tejana* (a Texas-style cowboy hat), the symbol of the *norteño*, the northern *mexicano*. The wearing of a *tejana*, what many would argue is symbolic practice, began when Don Roberto began frequenting Mexico. He worked in the produce industry until his death at the age of eighty-five in 2003 and traveled frequently to a variety of fruit regions throughout Mexico. Although he was the only person among his cohorts from Lemon Grove who donned the *tejana*, people from Lemon Grove embraced this symbol. It became a recognition of *mexicanidad* and a representation of success for the community.

In addition to the resurgence of *mexicanidad* in Lemon Grove, there are cases of Lemon Grove offspring crossing the border to live in Mexico. Such returns are not isolated events, and include the "return" of both first- and second-generation U.S. citizens to Mexico after adulthood and life in the United States.[3] Manuel Smith, like his father, Manuel Smith Mesa, was born in Baja California and became a police officer.[4] Manuel Sr. had been the first Mexican-American in the San Diego police force. Because of Manuel's knowledge of the border and of Spanish, he worked as a liaison for the Tijuana and San Diego police departments. He married and settled in San Diego, but he and his wife, a Mexican citizen, also established themselves in a ranch in En Valle de la Trinidad close to his father's birthplace. In El Valle, his uncle (and mine), Guillermo Simpson, had also bought a ranch. The fathers of Guillermo and Manuel had roamed this region of Baja California as young men, after the migration of their parents to the United States. Two important mines, El Real del Castillo and El Alamo, flourished in this area when the original pioneer migrants meandered north to San Diego. It was here that my great-grandparents, the Smiths, who were also Manuel's grandparents, first arrived, and it was here that Manuel's father was born.

The irony of "being" American meets the essence of identity. Manuel became a homicide detective and retired from the San Diego police force with honors. Although both his name (Smith) and his career and life in the United States bespeak the role and model of a "good American," Manuel takes pride in the fact that he and his family are *mexicano*, with a history of Mexican immigrants and a strong sentiment of *mexicanidad*. Manuel continues to live in San Diego, but he frequents the ranch in El Valle de la Trinidad. His sentiment and identity are tied to this place and its memories.

In my own life, I have come to know Mexico from differing per-suasions. As a scholar of the border, of Mexico, I initially wrote of the past and the present couched in the literary markers of the anthropo-logical. I grew up struggling to be an American, and at times shed my Mexicanness for recognition as a "regular" American high school stu-dent, a surfer, a "college man" in the strictest of stereotyped senses. As I grew to realize, however, that my role "changes" from *vato loco* (crazy dude) to American boy, from Bob to Roberto, essentializing the shifting patterns of socialization pressure, I also reconnected with a Mexican past and present.

Between 1984 and 1989, I worked in Tijuana—"on the border"— in the fruit trade, with my father. During that period, I discovered a cer-tain Mexicanness that I believed I had never denied, but in reality had never really known. Although I had grown up "on the border," experi-enced a lifelong engagement in the United States, and procured a Ph.D. with a focus on Mexico, I can say now that I had not fully experienced *mexicanidad*. The rekindling of identity tied to a Mexican reality in Baja California, in Tijuana, in Mexico, stirred my reidentification, not with a borderness, but with a certain Mexicanness.

Mexicanidad can be seen as more than a recognition and sense of identity; *mexicanidad* should be viewed as a process. Especially when viewed historically and with reference to specific places and specific communi-ties, the process of *mexicanidad* raises new and important questions.

Lemon Grove illustrates the importance of place. The sociologi-cal boundaries of U.S. society, the discrimination and forced "accultur-ation," serve at first to accentuate the need to identify with U.S. society. But then, as David Gutierrez illustrates in *Walls and Mirrors* (1995), eth-nic distinctiveness, in this case Mexican-American, is constantly *rein-forced* by discriminatory treatment, in Lemon Grove, Los Angeles, and the Southwest in general.

We must remember that the geopolitical border and Mexico have had differing influences in the borderlands. Joe Alcozer, a current resi-dent of San Diego, but born of Mexican parentage from Piedras Negras, tells of growing up in south Texas without ever entering Mexico until he joined the navy during World War II. Along with other Tejanos, he was shipped out of Texas on the railroad that passed into Baja California (Mexico) and into the small town of Tecate, before arriving in San Diego. Even today, Mexico does not evoke the identity of his past and present.

The variation of experience and histories in specific places of the borderlands indicates that the specific patterns of behavior and identity of people along the U.S.–Mexico border are closely tied to interpreted histories, cultural space, and social processes.[5]

Transnationalism beyond the Border

The world has undergone critical events in recent years that in some ways have ruptured the status quo of much of our thinking. The post-modern dilemma of the 1980s that challenged the boundary keeping of the social sciences alerted us to the complex questions of representation, of writing and presenting ethnography. Yet at the turn of the twenty-first century many anthropologists were still clinging to disciplinary and political approaches that have prevented a realistic engagement with the changing profiles of the everyday world. Caught in the balance of tired and increasingly irrelevant arguments concerning the definition of the discipline and its subject matter, we somehow continue to let the world go by.

Without doubt there is a cutting edge of the discipline, bringing in new ideas and interpretations. Yet anthropologists continue, as a discipline, to argue about the scientific measure and definition of specific constructs (culture, race, identity, ethnicity, power, agency, and so on). Their discussions of race, for example, negate racialized and racist structures, and obscure how such organizations and individuals continue to forge public opinion and nation-state policy. Their constructs have meaning not only for understanding social processes but in their interpretive use. The outcome has been a neutralized politic and provincialized disciplinary perception of how the anthropological defines the world.

The post-September 11, 2001, events alert us to the violations and intensification of nation-state intrusions into the lives of people all over the earth. Ethnicity, power, race, and identity take on intensified meaning in the processes on which anthropologists focus.

The dynamics of global and transnational processes are vividly foregrounded in the realities of national processes and local-level behavior. This is especially evident in the Latin American and Asian embrace of neoliberal trade and values, and the growing visibility of the U.S. involvement and investments in transnational economies and negotiations. The past decade has seen an explosion of transnational behavior that highlights the character of the new globalism. For example, the Mexican–U.S. mango market has incorporated not only South America, Central America, and the Caribbean (Brazil, Ecuador, Venezuela, Peru, Guatemala, Costa Rica, Haiti), but more recently the Philippines (which in 2002 was cleared for mango export into the United States). The distribution of mangos is part of a greater world market encompassing Australia, which ships mangos to China, and the Philippines, which exports to Japan, Hong Kong, and Singapore. Israel, India, and Pakistan ship mangos to the European Union, as do South Africa, the Ivory Coast, Mali, Burkina Faso, Gambia, Guinea, and Kenya. In Europe, Spanish growers are switching to market varieties for future trade (*Rap Market Information:* 2002).

This is truly a global phenomenon that raises questions not only about trade and economics, but also about the local-level responses and human conditions relating to production and distribution. It includes new technological processes that promise to open trade with countries striving to become part of the global marketplace. Like all transnational behavior, this is a circular process in which trade balances are sought by participating nations.

The ethnographic venues described in this book attempt to break into this broader, visible condition of the transnational. In addition to illustrating and fleshing out how people and the state engage the global, I would argue that although the transnational has become popular in both the social sciences and the media, we have yet to really understand how this global phenomenon works at the ground level. Transnationalism is often rhetorical in its usage—an "ism" that pervades and attaches to the global, in often imprecise ways. As in early migration theory where actors and agency were subsumed in the broad strokes of "push and pull" forces, transnationalism glosses the primary actions of people engaging the global. Transnational studies focus on current immigrant diasporas that connect homes in bilateral communities (Basch, Glick-Schiller, and Blanc-Szanton 1994). Yet the everyday behavior of people and institutions in global (i.e., transnational) activities is only beginning to surface in social-science research. This raises important questions about how people engage transnationalism. What is the daily social reality of the transnational? What economic, political, and cultural behaviors do people use to engage global/transnational capitalism and its institutions? What results are reflected in the practice, agency, and identity of people in transnational settings? People and commodities crossing international borders are crucial, but we also need to question the role of the nation-state in localized transnational behavior. The "transnational" often implies the mere crossing of borders of adjacent nations, as well as the movement of bodies through global space. This neglects the local processes in transnational activity that, I argue, are the normal human condition of the global age. The focus here has been on the specificity of individual and group strategies, on the importance of locales, on the meaning of space and place, which explicate history, cultural interpretation, and the particularities of individual agency.

Transnational behavior is varied, divergent, and specific and might be better viewed as a transnationality that goes beyond the mere crossing of international geopolitical borders. The markets of Los Angeles, *norteño* truckers, and border folks (Lemon Grove) bear witness to a diverse universe that is often glossed over in "transnationalism." Anthropologists acknowledge myriad processes and divergent activity of people engaged in global trade and immigration yet have failed to decipher differing transnationalities in this milieu. From this perspective, the transnational can be seen as the other side of the global coin, wherein the social and material particularities of capitalism are enacted, and acted upon, by people and institutions. It is here that the broader forces meet the creative agency of people. The examples presented in this book dissect the transnationalism so profoundly embedded in most of our global thinking. What particular activities define global transnationalism? we ask. How do difference and variation illuminate the workings and underbelly of capitalism, the new nationalism of the nation-state, and the profound encounters of the vast diasporas of the new millennium? Transnationality bears witness to the encompassing process at local levels that is part and parcel of the contemporary global context.

Anthropologists and most social scientists concede that people throughout the world are indeed engaged in global activities. The people we study have moved out of the peasant-traditionalist world and not only recognize, but participate in, a new cosmopolitanism enhanced and often designed by the mass media, and facilitated by the spread of neoliberal trade. Yet they fail to acknowledge that most people strive to enter entrepreneurial activities within which they actually engage in capitalistic endeavors. A focus on entrepreneurs who work through cultural filters and barriers illustrates the wide range and variety of behavior that is conditioned by capitalism, and is framed as transnational activity. These cultural nuances, as the logic of *la maroma* illustrates, are creative responses that include transnational repertoires that are shaped in new ways. *La maroma* includes market knowledge of faraway Los Angeles, but many of its practitioners may never cross the geopolitical line.

The notions of "the border" and "borderlands" are encompassed in the various ethno-transnational scenarios presented in this book. Although the concept of the border or borderlands is often subsumed in "the transnational," these terms are rarely uttered in the same phrase. The assumption is that people and commodities cross the geopolitical border, but the value-laden experiences of this crossing and the resultant strategies of transnational people are often left to the imagination. In this book, the geopolitical border between Mexico and the United States has great significance, but it is not "the border" per se that creates the transnational behavior. The multiple variations of reactions to the border are results of the conflicts of abutting nation-states. Reference to the border usually spurns discussions that center on the conflicts and contradictions of inequality, policy, control, and economics, to name a few important areas of concern. These conflicts relate specifically to the nation-state's historical underpinnings and the political agendas that have created the racialized class and gendered divisions in people, and continue to produce difference rather than harmony.

On some borders people do live cooperatively, regardless of the geopolitical line that separates nation-states (Wilson and Donnan 1998). Representing "the border" as solely conflicting and contrasting does injustice to examples of cooperative well-being for many living on both sides of the U.S.–Mexico border and to the efforts of institutions on either side of the political line. Oscar Martinez in *Border People* (1994) provides ample evidence of balanced lives of people who live "on the border" but experience their lives in both Mexico and the United States. The collaborative efforts by city and non-profit organizations in most "sister cities" along the two thousand–mile demarcation also exemplify cooperation (Ortiz-Gonzalez 2003). The racialized indifference and ideology that produce discrimination, unequal access to jobs, unfair labor practices, and poor housing are continuing problems that have reached crisis levels in some areas. But the borderland is a specific place and home to a large number of people where memory, place, and historical particularism define community and identity. As the case of my parents' generation in Lemon Grove illustrates, defining and claiming cultural space is linked to border life, but goes "beyond the border" in Mexican—not "bordered"—ways.

This does not diminish the existing and growing inequalities created by nation-state policy at the border. Indeed, the memories and (re)creation of cultural space in Mexico are in part the result of the discriminating and hierarchical tendencies of Mexican-American experiences on the border. Such inequality is pervasive along the entire border. One of the most curious features of this inequality is the fact that some of the poorest counties in the United States are found along the Mexican–U.S. border, populated primarily by people of Mexican descent, whereas on the Mexican side of the geopolitical line one finds the strongest economic areas in Mexico. This conundrum highlights the social contradictions that result from the national realities of the geopolitical in the borderlands.

The borderlands exemplify the face-to-face of transnational and global interactions of people in multisocial, political, cultural, and economic backgrounds. The borderlands occupy not only space, but also imagination. Geographically, the borderlands range spreads centrifugally from the geopolitical line; some authors claim, in an actual strip of specific mileage on either side of the political border, as if outside the borderland limits one sees a different world. But as illustrated by the markets of Los Angeles, the activities of people elude the spatial limitations of a border zone or an adjacent "borderlands" of the geopolitical line. Yet people confront the conflict and contradictions of social-cultural and economic survival in Los Angeles, as throughout the borderlands range, paralleling the conditions of people on the border itself. The truckers of the Mayan south and the *norteño* truckers offer a comparative instance of manipulation of the geopolitical border and the cultural borderlands. The geopolitical border is real, but so too are the cross-cultural, complex "global" scenarios experienced by these and other folks. In this case, the borderlands encompass the actual geopolitical line but also include those areas "beyond the border" where the conflict and ideologies of the state and capitalism continue to give rise to border strategies that encompass social-cultural repertoires and styles of people engaged in the transnational.

Identity in transnational studies has focused on the continuing relationships of immigrants to "home culture." There is no question that people do express allegiance and emotional ties to natal locations, but they also respond to the changing scenarios of global life in imaginative ways. Recall, for example, the Maya truckers who dress in *norteño* style while on the road, but return to the *huipil* of the Zinacanteco when in their home hamlets. They speak of being Zinacanteco and stress cultural ideologies to which they adhere, as does the trade-union leader who said he was "100 percent milpa farmer" even though farming was only a small part of his life. Such dynamics challenge the structured social-science paradigms that seek to explain how people express and construct identity. Like culture, identity is a construct of the social sciences that helps to explain and understand people's interactions and strategic behaviors. The concept of "an identity," like that of "a culture," continues to evade the reality of people's lives. Viewed through the examples presented in this book, identity is in part a process and repertoire that people build through experience and time. The changing perceptions of people throughout their life illustrate profound realizations and reconstructions of identity. Through the lives of my own parents' generation, for example, one can see a *long-term* recognition of *mexicanidad* as a significant and chosen part of being (identity). These people developed this recognition over time and through various life experiences, enhanced by the specific histories and memory of Lemon Grove. The social practice and social institutions described in this book illustrate how people produce identities and give them determinate social meaning. Similarly, the *comerciante* identity of *chileros* and *fruteros* of *la maroma* and the markets of Los Angeles are composed of a cultural style and an economic strategy that are embedded in a nationalistic sentiment of being Mexican. In my own experience, I entered the *chilero* world and incorporated the *frutero* ideology into my own repertoire, which also includes being *mexicano*, Chicano, American, anthropologist, teacher, husband, father, and son.

Identities are dynamically re-created every day under socially and historically specific circumstances. I recognize the institutions, practices, and ideas that shape the subjectivities of the actors on whom I focus. People shift and negotiate identities precisely for specific social and cultural circumstances and evoke specific identities in various situations. But they adhere to particular identities based on place, history, and belonging. The *remexicanizados* of Lemon Grove, like Zinacanteco truckers, exemplify an essential identity that illustrates not just how people act and represent themselves, but also how they define and claim belonging. This raises questions about how we recognize who we are, and under what types of circumstances we evoke our repertoires. Lemon Grove also illustrates a simple but crucial factor about identity: it changes over time. What is crucial in this regard are the broader hierarchical class and racial ideologies and practices that impinge on and often force particular identities.

The essence of time and history is a significant aspect of the transnational and borderlands realities discussed in this book. The eth-nographic vignettes provide short glimpses into larger transnational social fields that have come to light through long-term research. This is not an eclectic array of research interests but a time-enriched field of experiences that are tied together by researcher as participant. Each of the ethnographic examples stems from my own involvement in the com-munities and activities, not solely as a researcher but as an active player. The interaction of the various research sites and experiences produces relevant analytical descriptions and insight into changing processes. What is important is not my individual involvement, but the engage-ment of social-science researchers in the historical conditions and com-munities within which we work. Nearly a half century ago, C. Wright Mills in *The Sociological Imagination* urged social-science scholars to engage themselves in current history and extract the essence of the soci-ological present. This was a passionate plea to engage as scholars, and individuals, in the complexity of our times. As I read Mills, I believe this to be a holistic and encompassing dialogue enacted in the totality of our lives. This includes a long-term engagement that ultimately not only helps us understand our subjects, the social context and world we live in, but the nature of change and its effects on people and institutions. The example of Lemon Grove illustrates the dynamic of individual and "community" agency over time, as does the changing nature of Zinacan-teco accommodation to Mexican society and economics. Such relational changes not only reflect individual strategies but elucidate how broader policy such as NAFTA, U.S.–Mexico border control, global markets and institutional forms such as the nation-state contextualize and create new social environments in which people act.

Indeed, the work presented here encompasses broad historical and political-economic circumstances that affect individual and institutional behavior. Rather than viewing this context as a static background, here it is processual and ever changing with the particularities of human engagement and historical dynamics. Throughout this book, the trans-national is process-focused and variable, and dependent on social cir-cumstances, cultural foundations, and historical dynamics, as well as on place and how it is defined and claimed by individuals. The transnational is not a form of global action, but rather a product of interchange and the strategic behavior of people in local settings. Thus context is more than the societal constraints and structural parameters of the political and the economic. Context is interactive rather than deterministic, exerting differing protocols among different sets of social-cultural fields.

The example of ethnic chile entrepreneurs who practice *la maroma* illustrates how local-level social organization works, but also how it is part of a greater hemispheric process engendered by capital, finance, and markets. The everyday strategies of business are contoured to existing resources and the broader, often invisible, influences of banking (finance) and the nation-state. The mango market exhibits similar but unique conditions of distribution directly tied to nation-state control and involvement, large capital investment, and technological necessity. In the context of the North American Free Trade Agreement, these activities in the Mexican–U.S. mango trade, and among *chileros*, illustrate the social-cultural interpenetration of global trade and neoliberal effects among people on the ground.

The nation-state—often viewed as a monolithic in-place phenomenon—is an actor that engages the transnational. It exacts control and extends its influence and power to neighboring nations across the geopolitical divide. This control extends beyond the border in multiple ways. The Border Patrol is a good example (Lytle-Hernandez 2002; Schaus 2000), as are the USDA and Customs. Importantly, this type of activity is different from the activities of the U.S. State Department and the Department of Defense in which the uses of the U.S. state's political and ideological apparatus in war and power take on a global dimension. The transnationalism discussed in this book reflects more subtle but equally significant nation-state incursions into nonthreatening areas such as the marketing of fruits and vegetables. Nevertheless, these types of activities have profound affects.

Of crucial importance is the identification and recording of immigrant and ethnic contributions to the global and the U.S. economy. Throughout this book, people have been shown to define their activities

through creative action and social strategy. These efforts not only reflect individual strategies but play a role in the broader economy in
which they are embedded. The mango market, for example, is more than
an ethnic niche market. It strongly influences broader trade processes,
nation-state policies, and hemispheric immigration patterns. The challenge to trade and immigration policy is not often viewed from the
perspective of small-scale entrepreneurs or distributors, but these actors
are crucial to the workings of larger economic incentives. The *chileros*
(who practice *la maroma*), the U.S. mango market, the *fruteros* of the Los
Angeles market, and the truckers of both the south and the north of
Mexico underscore not only the emergent and culturally productive
processes through which each set of entrepreneurs extends ethnicity, but
the economic engagement of new markets and social endeavors. The
growth of the ethnic markets in the United States has spawned a significant import–export trade, which for Mexico and the United States is a
significant factor in trade relations. These ethnic markets, growing out
of the dramatic increase in new immigrants in the United States (as in
Europe) have propelled new techniques in global fruit and vegetable
processing and distribution. The seemingly unimportant role of truckers, for example, is not often viewed from the perspective of global distribution, yet the huge volume of fruit and vegetables exported into
the United States from Mexico, which find their way onto grocery-store
shelves and nonimmigrant American tables, is driven to market by independent and company *troqueros*.

Truckers form part of this trade and virtually embody the nuances
of globalism and transnationalism in their mobility and connection to
various nodes of production and distribution. Such informal sectors are
important foci not only for identifying the labor exploitation and racialized ideologies that affect ethnic populations, but also for understanding
their culturally mediated lifestyles in relation to dominant, often exploitative and racialized structures. Truckers set trends in popular culture by
carrying music and new cultural trends between differing domains. For
example, Zinacanteco truckers redefine the domain in which Mayas
conduct their lives as ethnic peoples and expand the territorial boundaries

of community, especially for women. This activity forms the social basis of the transnational and contributes to the creation of stable and enduring economic sectors.

The Los Angeles market is a transnational social-scape that illustrates the results of such ethnic enterprise. The market and its *fruteros* illustrate how transnational information flows really work as immigrants and *fruteros* arrive with specific skills and knowledge of products and the market. The various jobs and the hierarchy of the market itself illustrate the great diversity and the long-range maintenance of transnational ties that foster commerce and recruit labor and knowledgeable actors. In this endeavor, creativity and engagement are crucial. They can be seen in the accommodation of new settlers and in the creative use of knowledge from a variety of social-cultural worlds. This *is* transnationalism in everyday practice.

These processes open up many possibilities for future research sites and questions and challenge our views about the interpretation of the transnational. What, for instance, is the historical significance of specific instances of transnational behavior? Is all transnational behavior a result of global capitalism? How do we explain and describe the creative process of recurring, reemergent ethnic identity? What new roles and activities do people develop that go beyond a simple reorientation and commitment to cultural nationality and regional ties? And what can the current experience and interpretations of people tell us about the changing nature and future possibilities of transnational process and globalism? Such an inquiry will not only help us to understand the ways people respond to nation-state force and hierarchy, but also to meet such force in better and more creative ways.

Notes

Foreword

1. Immanuel Wallerstein et al., *Open the Social Sciences: Report of the Gulbenkian Commission on the Restructuring of the Social Sciences* (Standford, CA: Stanford University Press, 1996), 94–95.

2. Carlos Fuentes, *A New Time for Mexico* (Berkeley: University of California Press, 1997), xiii.

3. Earl Lewis, *In Their Own Interests* (Berkeley: University of California Press, 1989).

4. Stephanie De La Torre and Adrian Arancibia, eds., *Chorizo Tonguefire: The Taco Shop Poets Anthology* (San Diego: Chorizo Tonguefire Press, 1999), 15. The taco shop poets are a collective from San Diego committed to moving poetry out of the coffee shops and into the taco shops.

1. Beyond the Border

1. The focus on process, and in particular the mango export system, stems from concerns I have had about the U.S.–Mexico border and the social organization of Mexican export trade (Alvarez 1991, 1994, 1998) and specifically studies of the borderlands (Alvarez 1995). I, like others (Wilson and Donnan 1998; Cook 1998; Heyman 1995) argue that it is time to state our concerns and proceed with focused ethnographic reconnaissance of the border. We have moved beyond the rhetorical metaphors of border crossings and mixed identities and need now to focus on specific social processes in border behavior (see, for example, Cook 1998). These are problems associated with the influence of the actual

123

geopolitical border, but force us beyond the boundaries of the local to investigate the systemic processes of border control in the globalized world (Gupta and Ferguson 1996). Such views of the local and the global are becoming more crucial (Alvarez 1998; Barros-Nock 1998).

3. The Long Haul in Mexican Trucking

This chapter was originally published as an article coauthored with George A. Collier in *American Ethnologist* 21, no. 3 (1994): 606–27. The research for this study was facilitated in part by support to George A. Collier from the National Science Foundation, Grant BNS-8804607, for the study of "Agrarian Change in Southeastern Mexico," and from the Consortium of International Earth Sciences Information Network for the study of "Deforestation, Land Use, and Development in the Greater Mayan Region." We thank Frank Cancian, Jane F. Collier, Akhil Gupta, Rosalva Aída Hernández, Elena Lazos, Bill Maurer, Roger Noll, Stuart Plattner, Jan Rus, and John Young for critical advice and commentary. Truckers are not the only Zinacantecos who provide transport for their compatriots. Zinacantecos also run a fleet of *combis* (VW Microbuses) that provide regular transport along routes connecting hamlets to San Cristóbal de Las Casas and to the Zinacantán municipal center. The *combi* transport, which is organized similarly to that of trucking, also affords ethnic compatriots with transport for goods and people.

1. Ambiguities of class position are increasingly apparent throughout rural Mexico. Investigators find that "peasants" mix farming with salaried wage work and independent small enterprise in extremely varied ways. Collier (1990, 1992) describes how oil development has drawn highland Maya peasants into increasingly differentiated and varied productive relations.

2. We do not treat shippers of produce involved in transport primarily for North American-based agribusiness corporations such as Dole, Campbell Soup, Del Monte, or General Foods, all of which operate in Mexico. Our focus is rather on independent shippers who supply wholesale produce markets.

3. The advent of NAFTA and the reform of Article 27 of the Mexican Constitution to allow for privatization of the *ejido* may eliminate smallholders and *ejidatarios* in favor of more concentrated landholding and production.

4. INI promoted trucking in conjunction with "cooperatives" that in fact enabled power holders in many communities to control businesses, for example, the distribution of liquor in Chamula and of soft drinks in Chamula and Zinacantán (Crump 1987; Wasserstrom 1983; see also Nash's [1985, 86–87] discussion of the role of trucking in factional politics related to the transport of artisanal pottery in Amatenango del Valle; and Loyola's 1988 dissertation on the development of trucking in Tenejapa).

5. Zinacanteco truckers are not homogeneous. A few truckers, for example, ship only soft drinks, for which bottling firms grant them monopolies of transport to specific hamlets. These businesses are more lucrative than farming, but they are exceptional because of the monopolies that sustain them.

6. Although merchants buy and sell products on a cash basis, some do buy corn, fruit, and other produce prior to harvest at a discount, thereby assuming some risk of nondelivery and some speculative possibility of profit or loss if the price of the commodity changes unexpectedly. This practice is not uncommon in the marketing of orchard crops in other regions of Mexico, but in the south it is conceptualized as an alternative to the producer's taking out a loan at interest.

7. Loyola (1988, 174) reports that the Mexican government granted a specific trucking firm the monopoly of shipping fertilizer from the national distributor to communities in central and eastern Chiapas that needed fertilizer for coffee production. Zinacantán is much closer to distributing warehouses than Tenejapa and the other communities to which Loyola refers, and Zinacantecos have been able to take delivery of fertilizer at the warehouses.

8. A variety of transport is available in the regional economy of central Chiapas, including local and long-distance bus and taxi service. These services are nonetheless less convenient—and often less pleasant—for villagers to use than the transport services that originate in their own communities.

9. It is becoming evident from the comparison of different migrant-sending populations, for example, those involved in circuits extending north from Michoacán (Rouse 1991) as compared to Mixtecs from Oaxaca (Kearney 1988; Nagengast and Kearney 1990), that these populations also carry with them and elaborate distinctive styles of organization (e.g., family network versus collective) in their experience of exploitative labor in the borderlands.

5. Los Remexicanizados

1. Interview with Antonio Urcino Alvarez Castellanos, January 4, 2000, Phoenix, Arizona.

2. Ibid.

3. For example see Martinez (1994) and Vélez-Ibáñez (1996).

4. The Smiths are primarily from the town of Comundu in the state of Baja California del Sur, Mexico. English and other European surnames are common in this part of the state because of early settlers who came with the whale and sea-otter trade during the mid- to late 1800s.

5. Interview with Joe Alcozer, San Diego, March 14, 2000. His motivation for joining the service was "to show the Americans we were as good as them." Throughout his life, he worked for social equality as a union leader for *mexicanos* in San Diego County. He was also instrumental in founding the Don Diego Post of the Veterans of Foreign Wars in San Diego. The profoundness of the subjectivity of local people's behavior in the general milieu of the borderlands is also illustrated by Oscar Martinez's *Border People* (1994). Martinez goes to great lengths in classifying and typologizing this complexity.

Works Cited

Acheson, James. 1985. "Social Organization of the Maine Lobster Market." In *Markets and Marketing*, ed. Stuart Plattner, 105–32. Lanham, MD: University Press of America.

Adams, Richard. 1970. "Brokers and Career Mobility Systems in the Structure of Complex Societies." *Southwestern Journal of Anthropology* 26: 315–27.

Agar, Michael H. 1986. *Independents Declared: The Dilemmas of Independent Trucking.* Washington, DC: Smithsonian Institution Press.

Alvarez, Robert R. 1986. "The Lemon Grove Incident: The Nation's First Successful Desegregation Court Case." *Journal of San Diego History* 32 (Spring): 116–36.

———. 1987. *Familia: Migration and Adaptation in Alta and Baja California, 1800–1975.* Berkeley: University of California Press.

———. 1989. "Chileros: Mexican and American Entrepreneurs in the Border Economy." Paper presented to the Department of Anthropology, Arizona State University, Tempe.

———. 1990. "Mexican Entrepreneurs and Markets in the City of Los Angeles: The Case of an Ethnic Enclave." *Urban Anthropology* 19(1): 99–124.

———. 1991 [1987]. *Familia, Migration and Adaptation in Alta and Baja California, 1850–1975.* Berkeley: University of California Press.

———. 1994. "Changing Ideology in a Transnational Market: Chiles and Chileros in Mexico and the U.S." *Human Organization* 53(3): 255–62.

———. 1995. "The Mexican–U.S. Border: The Making of an Anthropology of Borderlands." *Annual Review of Anthropology* 24: 447–70.

———. 1998. "La Maroma: Chile, Credit, and Chance: An Ethnographic Case of Global Finance Middlemen Entrepreneurs." *Human Organization* 57(1): 63–73.

Alvarez, Robert, and George A. Collier. 1994. "The Long Haul in Mexican Trucking: Traversing the Borderlands of the North and the South." *American Ethnologist* 21(3): 606–27.

Anzaldúa, Gloria. 1987. *Borderlands, La Frontera: The New Mestiza.* San Francisco: Spinsters/Aunt Lute.

Appadurai, Arjun. 1986. "Introduction: Commodities and the Politics of Value." In *The Social Life of Things: Commodities in Cultural Perspective.* London: Cambridge University Press.

———. 1990. "Disjuncture and Difference in the Global Cultural Economy." In *Global Culture: Nationalism, Globalization and Modernity,* ed. Mike Featherstone. Newbury Park, CA: Sage Publications.

———. 1996. *Modernity at Large: Cultural Dimensions of Globalization.* Minneapolis: University of Minnesota Press.

Babb, Florence. 1985. "Middlemen and 'Marginal' Women: Marketers and Dependency in Peru's Informal Sector." In *Markets and Marketing,* ed. Stuart Plattner, 287–308. Lanham, MD: University Press of America.

Banamex. 1993. *Review of the Economic Situation of Mexico* 69(810) (May).

Barros-Nock, Magdalena. 1998. "Small Farmers in the Global Economy: The Case of the Fruit and Vegetable Business in Mexico." Ph.D. dissertation. Institute of Social Studies, The Hague, the Netherlands.

Basch, Linda, Nina Glick-Schiller, and Cristina Blanc-Szanton. 1994. *Nations Unbound: Transnational Projects, Postcolonial Predicaments, and Deterritorialized Nation-States.* Basel: Gordon and Breach International.

Bonacich, Edna. 1973. "A Theory of Middleman Minorities." *American Sociological Review* 38: 583–94.

Bonacich, Edna, and John Modell. 1980. "Middlemen Minorities." In *The Economic Basis of Ethnic Solidarity: Small Business in the Japanese American Community.* Berkeley: University of California Press.

Bourdieu, Pierre. 1977. *Outline of a Theory of Practice.* Cambridge: Cambridge University Press.

Braudel, Fernand. 1980. "History and the Social Sciences: *The Longue Durée.*" In *On History,* 25–55. Chicago: University of Chicago Press.

Buckley, Katherine C. 1990. *The World Market in Fresh Fruits and Vegetables, Wine and Tropical Beverages—Government Intervention and Multilateral Policy*

Reform. Commodity Economics Division, Economic Research Service. Washington, DC: United States Department of Agriculture.

Bunnin, Nicolas. 1963. "La industria de las flores en Zinacantán." In *Los Zinacantecos: Un pueblo Tzotzil de los altos de Chiapas,* ed. Evon Z. Vogt, 208–32. *Colección de Antropología Social,* 7. Mexico City: Instituto Nacional Indigenista.

Byrne, Daniel. 1985. "Economic Rationality in a Competitive Marketplace: When to Mix Apples and Oranges." In *Markets and Marketing,* ed. Stuart Plattner. Lanham, MD: University Press of America.

Canclini, Néstor García. 1995. *Hybrid Cultures: Strategies for Entering and Leaving Modernity.* Trans. Christopher L. Chiappar and Silvia L. López. Minneapolis: University of Minnesota Press.

Clifford, James, and George E. Marcus. 1984. *Writing Culture.* Berkeley: University of California Press.

Collier, George A. 1988. "Peasant Politics and the Mexican State: Indigenous Compliance in Highland Chiapas." *Mexican Studies/Estudios Mexicanos* 3(1): 71–98.

———. 1990. "Seeking Food and Seeking Money: Changing Productive Relations in a Highland Mexican Community." *Discussion Paper 11.* Geneva: United Nations Research Institute for Social Development.

———. 1992. "Búsqueda de alimentos o búsqueda de dinero: Cambios en las relaciones de producción en Zinacantán, Chiapas." In *Restructuración económica y subsistencia rural: El maíz y la crisis de los ochenta,* ed. Cynthia Hewitt de Alcántara, 183–221. Mexico City: El Colegio de México.

Cook, Scott. 1984. *Peasant Capitalist Industry: Piecework and Enterprise in Southern Mexican Brickyards.* Lanham, MD: University Press of America.

———. 1998. *The Mexican Brick Building Industry.* Dallas: Texas A and M Press.

Cook, Scott, and Leigh Binford. 1990. *Obliging Need: Rural Petty Industry in Mexican Capitalism.* Austin: University of Texas Press.

Crump, Thomas. 1987. "The Alternative Economy of Alcohol in the Chiapas Highlands." In *Constructive Drinking: Perspectives on Drink from Anthropology,* ed. Mary Douglas, 239–49. New York: Cambridge University Press.

Dosal, Paul J. 1993. *Doing Business with the Dictators.* Wilmington, DE: Scholarly Resources.

Edmonson, Munro S. 1959. *The Mexican Truck Driver.* New Orleans: Middle American Research Institute.

Empacadoras de Mango de Exportación. 2003. www.mangoemex.org.mx.

Fernández-Kelly, María Patricia. 1983. "Mexican Border Industrialization, Female Labor Force Participation, and Migration." In *Women, Men and the International Division of Labor*, ed. June Nash and María Patricia Fernández-Kelly. Albany: State University of New York Press.

Flynn, Donna K. 1997. "'We Are the Border': Identity, Exchange, and the State along the Benin–Nigeria Border." *American Ethnologist* 24(2): 311–54.

Frank, Andre Gunder. 1969. *Capitalism and Underdevelopment in Latin America*. New York: Monthly Review Press.

Fuentes, Carlos. 1986. *Christopher Unborn*. New York: Farrar, Straus and Giroux.

Garreau, Joel. 1981. *The Nine Nations of North America*. New York: Houghton-Mifflin.

Geertz, Clifford. 1978. "The Bazaar Economy: Information and Search in Peasant Marketing." *American Economic Review* 68: 28–32.

Gómez-Peña, Guillermo. 1987. "Wacha esa border, son." *La Jornada Semanal* (Mexico City) (October 25): 3–5.

Gupta, Akhil, and James Ferguson. 1992. "Beyond 'Culture': Space, Identity, and the Politics of Difference." *Cultural Anthropology* 7(1): 6–23.

———. 1996. *Culture, Power and Place*. Durham, NC: Duke University Press.

Gutierrez, David G. 1995. *Walls and Mirrors: Mexican Americans, Mexican Immigrants, and the Politics of Ethnicity*. Berkeley: University of California Press.

Hamel, Ruth, and Tim Schreiner. 1988. "Chile Pepper Market." *American Demographics* 10: 54.

Hannerz, Ulf. 1990. "Cosmopolitans and Locals in World Culture." In *Global Culture: Nationalism, Globalization and Modernity*, ed. Mike Featherstone. Newbury Park, CA: Sage Publications.

Hansen, Nels, and Gilberto Cardenas. 1988. "Immigrant and Native Ethnic Enterprises in Mexican American Neighborhoods: Differing Perceptions of Mexican Immigrant Workers." *International Migration Review* 22(2): 226–42.

Heyman, Josiah M. 1995. "The Mexico–U.S. Border in Anthropology: A Critique and Reformulation." *Journal of Political Ecology* 1(1): 43–65.

Horcasitas, Víctor. 1988. El estudio UNPH. Problemática de la exportación de frutas y legumbres mexicanas a Estados Unidos y Canadá. Mexico City: Unión Nacional de Productores de Hortalizas.

Hughes, William F., and James T. Peach. 1985. *Some Implications of the 1984 Tandem*

Truck Safety Act for the United States–Mexico Border Area. Borderlands Research Monograph Series 2. Las Cruces: New Mexico State University.

Jaquith, James R. 1974. *Gringos No . . . Gringas Sí: Ritual Expressions of Mexican Trucking. Museum of Anthropology Miscellaneous Series* 35. Greeley: Museum of Anthropology, University of Northern Colorado.

Kainuma, Koji. 1997. "Economic Competitiveness of the Western Mango Industry." Unpublished Master of Science thesis. University of Arizona, Tucson.

Kearney, Michael. 1988. "Mixtec Political Consciousness: From Active to Passive Resistance." In *Rural Revolt in Mexico and U.S. Intervention,* ed. Daniel Nugent. Monograph 27, Center for U.S.–Mexican Studies. San Diego: University of California Press.

———. 1998. *Reconceptualizing the Peasantry: Anthropology in Global Perspective.* Boulder, CO: Westview Press.

Langley, Lester D., and Thomas Schoonover. 1995. *The Banana Men: American Mercenaries and Entrepreneurs in Central America, 1880–1930.* Lexington: University of Kentucky Press.

Light, Ivan, and Edna Bonacich. 1988. *Immigrant Entrepreneurs: Koreans in Los Angeles.* Berkeley: University of California Press.

Lomnitz, Larissa. 1982. "Horizontal and Vertical Relations and the Social Structure of Urban Mexico." *Latin American Research Review* 17(2): 51–74.

Long-Solis, Janet. 1986. *Capsicum y cultura: La historia del Chile.* Mexico City: Fondo de Cultura Económica.

Loyola, Luis Jaime. 1988. "Accumulation and Development: Transporters in the Process of Economic and Political Change in Chiapas, Mexico." Ph.D. dissertation, City University of New York.

Lytle-Hernandez, Kelly. 2002. "Entangling Bodies and Borders: Racial Profiling and the U.S. Border Patrol, 1924–1955." Ph.D. dissertation, Department of History, University of California, Los Angeles.

Martinez, Oscar. 1994. *Border People: Life and Society in the U.S.–Mexico Borderlands.* Tucson: University of Arizona Press.

McLaughlin, B. 1993. *Linguistic, Psychological and Contextual Factors in Language Shift.* Santa Barbara: University of California Linguistics Minority Research Institute.

McMichael, Philip. 1995. "Introduction: Agrarian and Food Relations in the World Economy." In *Food and Agrarian Orders in the World-Economy,* ed. P. McMichael, ix–xvi. Westport, CT: Greenwood Press.

Mills, C. Wright. 1959. *The Sociological Imagination*. New York: Oxford University Press.

Mintz, Sidney. 1961. "Pratik: Haitian Personal Economic Relationships." In *Proceedings of the 1961 Annual Spring Meeting of the American Ethnological Society*. Washington, DC: American Anthropological Association.

Morales, Aurora Levins. 1995. "Child of the Americas." In Aurora Levins Morales and Rosario Morales. *Getting Home Alive*, Ithaca, NY: Firebrand Books, 1986. Reprinted in *Boricuas: Influential Puerto Rican Writings—An Anthology*, ed. Roberto Santiago, 79. New York: One World/Ballantine Books.

Nagengast, Carole, and Michael Kearney. 1990. "Mixtec Identity: Social Identity, Political Consciousness, and Political Activism." *Latin American Research Review* 25(2): 61–91.

Nash, June. 1985 [1970]. *In the Eyes of the Ancestors: Belief and Behavior in a Mayan Community*. Prospect Heights, NJ: Waveland Press.

———. 1993. *Crafts in the World Market: The Impact of Global Exchange on Middle American Artisans*. Albany: State University of New York Press.

Olson, F. J. 1988. *Briefing Paper*. San Diego: USDA-APHIS-Plant Protection and Quarantine.

Ong, Aihwa. 1987. *Spirits of Resistance and Capitalist Discipline*. Albany: State University of New York Press.

———. 1992. "Limits to Cultural Accumulation: Chinese Capitalists on the American Rim." In *Towards a Transnational Perspective on Migration*, ed. Nina Glick-Schiller, Linda Basch, and Cristina Blanc-Szanton. New York: New York Academy of Sciences.

Ortiz-Gonzalez, Victor M. 2003. *El Paso: Local Frontiers at a Global Crossroads*. Minneapolis: University of Minnesota Press.

Plattner, Stuart. 1982. "Economic Decision Making in a Public Marketplace." *American Ethnological Society* 9: 399–420.

———. 1983. "Economic Custom in a Competitive Marketplace." *American Anthropologist* 84: 848–58.

———. 1984. "Economic Decision Making of Marketplace Merchants: An Ethnographic Model." *Human Organization* 43(3): 252–64.

———. 1985a. "Equilibrating Market Relationships." In *Markets and Marketing*, ed. Stuart Plattner, 133–52. Lanham, MD: University Press of America.

———1985b. *Markets and Marketing. Monographs in Economic Anthropology*, no.

4. Society for Economic Anthropology. Lanham, MD: University Press of America.

———. 1989. "Markets and Marketplaces." In *Economic Anthropology*, ed. Stuart Plattner, 171–208. Stanford, CA: Stanford University Press.

Portes, Alejandro, and Robert L. Bach. 1985. *Latin Journey: Cuban and Mexican Immigrants in the United States*. Berkeley: University of California Press.

Produce Reporting Company. 1988. *Semiannual Blue Book Credit and Marketing Guide*. 123d ed. Wheaton, IL: Produce Reporting Co.

Rap Market Information. 2002. "World Market for Mango." Bulletin no. 9. www.agribusinessonline.com.

Rosaldo, Renato I. 1985. "Ideology, Place, and People without Culture." *Cultural Anthropology* 3: 77–87.

———. 1989. *Culture and Truth: The Remaking of Social Analysis*. Boston: Beacon Press.

Rothe, J. Peter. 1991. *The Trucker's World: Risk, Safety and Mobility*. New Brunswick, NJ: Transaction Publishers.

Rouse, Roger. 1991. "Mexican Migration and the Social Space of Postmodernism." *Diaspora* 1(1): 8–23.

Sanchez, George. 1993. *Becoming Mexican American*. Oxford: Oxford University Press.

Sassen-Koob, Saskia. 1982. "Recomposition and Peripheralization at the Core." *Contemporary Marxism* 5: 88–100.

———. 1983. "Labor Migration and the New Industrial Division of Labor." In *Women, Men and the International Division of Labor*, ed. June Nash and María Patricia Fernández-Kelly. Albany: State University of New York Press.

Schaus, Noel. 2000. "The Chandler Coalition on Civil Rights and Latino Cultural Citizenship." Unpublished MA paper. Department of Anthropology, Arizona State University.

Smith, Carol A. N.d. "Race/Class/Gender Ideology in Guatemala: 'Modern,' Nonmodern, and Revolutionary Forms." Working paper, Department of Anthropology, University of California, Davis.

———. 1985. "How to Count Onions: Methods for a Regional Analysis of Marketing." In *Markets and Marketing*, ed. Stuart Planner, 49–79. Lanham, MD: University Press of America.

Stanford, Lois. 1994. "Transitions to Free Trade: Local Impacts of Changes in Mexican Agrarian Policy." *Human Organization* 53(2): 99–109.

Tropical Produce Marketing News. 1996. "U.S. Mango Imports Keep Setting Records." Web site, April–May.

U.S. Bureau of the Census. 1983. *Census of Population and Housing: 1980, General Population Characteristics*. Washington, DC: U.S. Government Printing Office.

———. 2005. *Fact Sheet. Census 2000. Demographic Profile Highlights*. Web page: http://www.factfinder.census. Los Angeles County.

United States Department of Agriculture. 1983. "Los Angeles Fresh Fruit and Vegetable Wholesale Market Prices 1983." California Department of Food and Agriculture. Los Angeles: Bureau of Market News.

———. 1984. "Los Angeles Fresh Fruit and Vegetable Wholesale Market Prices 1984." California Department of Food and Agriculture. Los Angeles: Bureau of Market News.

———. 1985. "Los Angeles Fresh Fruit and Vegetable Wholesale Market Prices 1985." California Department of Food and Agriculture. Los Angeles: Bureau of Market News.

———. 1986. "Los Angeles Fresh Fruit and Vegetable Wholesale Market Prices 1986." California Department of Food and Agriculture. Los Angeles: Bureau of Market News.

———. 1987. "Los Angeles Fresh Fruit and Vegetable Wholesale Market Prices 1987." California Department of Food and Agriculture. Los Angeles: Bureau of Market News.

———. 1988. "Los Angeles Fresh Fruit and Vegetable Wholesale Market Prices 1988." California Department of Food and Agriculture. Los Angeles: Bureau of Market News.

United States Department of Agriculture-APHIS. 1990. *Guidelines on Preclearance and Related Programs*. Hyattsville, MD: USDA-APHIS.

———. 1993a. *Certifying Facilities: Hot Water Immersion Tanks*. Hoboken, NJ: USDA-APHIS.

———. 1993b. *Equipment for Hot Water Treatment of Mangoes*. Hoboken, NJ: USDA-APHIS.

———. 1993c. *Protocol for Approving New Hot Water Mango Treatment Facilities in Countries Wishing to Export Mangoes to the United States*. Hoboken, NJ: USDA-APHIS.

———.1994a. *Directory of Manufacturers, Suppliers, Engineering Firms and Consultants for Mango Hot Water Treatment Facilities*. Hoboken, NJ: USDA-APHIS.

———. 1994b. *Summary of Regulations Governing the Entry of Mangoes into the United States, and Quarantine Treatment Schedules That Apply*. Hoboken, NJ: USDA-APHIS.

United States Department of Agriculture Marketing Services. 1997. 1968–1997 *Annual Reports*. Nogales, AZ: USDA.

Velazquez De La Cadena, Mariano, Edward Gray, and Juan Iribas. 1972. *Dictionary of the Spanish and English Languages*. New York: Appleton.

Vélez-Ibáñez, Carlos G. 1983. *Bonds of Mutual Trust: The Cultural Systems of Rotating Credit Associations among Urban Mexicans and Chicanos*. New Brunswick, NJ: Rutgers University Press.

———. 1996. *Border Visions: Mexican Cultures of the Southwest United States*. Tucson: University of Arizona Press.

Vigil, James Diego, 1997. *Personas Mexicanas: Changing High Schoolers in a Changing Los Angeles*. Case Studies in Cultural Anthropology. New York: Harcourt Brace College Publishers.

Wallerstein, Immanuel. 1974. *The Modern World System: Capitalist Agriculture and the Origins of the European World-Economy in the Sixteenth Century*. New York: Academic Press.

Wassertrom, Robert. 1983. *Class and Society in Central Chiapas*. Berkeley: University of California Press.

Wells, Meriam J. 1996. *Strawberry Fields: Politics, Class and Work in California Agriculture*. Ithaca, NY: Cornell University Press.

Williams, Brackette F. 1989. "A Class Act: Anthropology and the Race to Nation across Ethnic Terrain." *Annual Review of Anthropology* 18: 401–44.

———. 1991. *Stains on My Name, War in My Veins*. Durham, NC: Duke University Press.

Wilson, James A. 1980. "Adaptation to Uncertainty and Small Numbers Exchange: The New England Fresh Fish Market." *Bell Journal of Economics* 11(2): 491–504.

Wilson, Thomas M., and Hastings Donnan. 1998. *Border Identities: Nation and State at International Frontiers*. Cambridge: Cambridge University Press.

Index

Robert R. Alvarez Jr. is professor in the Department of Ethnic Studies, University of California, San Diego. He grew up along the U.S.–Mexico border and worked in the Mexican produce industry. He is the author of *Familia: Migration and Adaptation in Alta and Baja California, 1850–1975.*